SHAKESPEARE'S
ART

THE TUPPER LECTURES
ON SHAKESPEARE
sponsored by
THE GEORGE WASHINGTON UNIVERSITY

SHAKESPEARE'S
ART/*Seven Essays*

Edited & with an Introduction by
MILTON CRANE

Published for
THE GEORGE WASHINGTON UNIVERSITY *by*
THE UNIVERSITY OF CHICAGO PRESS
Chicago & London

THE UNIVERSITY OF CHICAGO PRESS, CHICAGO 60637
THE UNIVERSITY OF CHICAGO PRESS, LTD., LONDON
© 1973 BY THE GEORGE WASHINGTON UNIVERSITY
All rights reserved. Published 1973
Printed in the United States of America
International Standard Book Number: 0-226-11835-5
Library of Congress Catalog Card Number: 72-92853

Contents

Introduction

Fred S. Tupper, in whose honor the essays in this volume were written, dedicated his professional life to the study and the teaching of English literature. More particularly, he brought to generations of students a rich and exciting awareness of the plays and poems of William Shakespeare.

No one can say precisely how a literary artist long dead and a young student beginning his experience of the arts become elective affinities. But few would doubt—and those of us who teach must surely believe—that in this extraordinary process the personality of the teacher, and the contagion of his own enthusiasm and love for the poet whom he interprets, play a vital role. Fred Tupper clearly was such a catalyst. Eight years after his final illness prematurely ended his career at The George Washington University, its community remains fully conscious of his influence on students and colleagues alike. And the university counts it among its own achievements that Fred Tupper, and men and women of his kind, have chosen to make that community their permanent professional home.

When colleagues, former associates, and grateful students cast about for a fitting memorial that The George Washington University might raise to Fred Tupper the teacher and critic, it seemed eminently natural that they should turn to the idea of a series of lectures on Shakespeare, who had been the focus of so much of his work and his interest. As a result of their effort—an unusual one in the history of the university—an outstanding man or woman from the world of Shakespeare criticism and scholarship has been brought here in April of each year to give a public lecture at the university in honor of Fred Tupper, to which the entire academic and nonacademic community of this city is invited. The alumni, and above all the university administration, have been unstinting in their support of this undertaking, and the Annual Tupper Lecture is today a significant date on the university's calendar.

This book is not a festschrift in the usual sense of the word: one would look in vain here for the homogeneity or special focus that characterizes contributions commissioned for a single occasion and centered around the person and the work of the one being honored, often in his lifetime. The Tupper essays may be said to have only two unifying elements: they are yet another monument to Shakespeare, and they grew out of the wish to honor a man who taught Shakespeare's art.

In a larger sense, of course, the contributors have more in common. They share with one another the joyful awareness that those of us who are allowed to devote much of our lives to Shakespeare (as other groups of scholars devote themselves to Homer, Sophocles, Dante, or Goethe) are greatly privileged. Indeed, it hardly requires the classroom or the lecture platform to remind us—overpoweringly at times—of the extent to which Shakespeare dominates, enriches, and informs the language of our daily life. To have achieved this unrivaled impact, which transcends the barriers of class, time, and even national language, the poet, we tend to agree, must himself have known life as intimately as none before or after him. Yet how a single being could have combined in himself Shakespeare's art, his wisdom, and his detailed knowledge of the ways of man remains the ever-challenging question, an answer to which has thus far eluded the questers. Bernard Shaw imagined Shakespeare as an Elizabethan Henry Higgins, snapping up unconsidered poetic trifles on his nocturnal walks through London. We may not want to go quite so far as Shaw, but somewhere, we suspect, the playwright and the beefeater must have met and exchanged words and so established one of the abiding Shakespeare legends.

Such generalizations aside, the richness of the Tupper essays lies in their very diversity. Their authors represent not only the finest in the field of Shakespeare study but a great variety of schools and persuasions within it.

From the outset, the subjects of the essays here included were chosen by the authors themselves upon their acceptance of the university's invitation to deliver the annual address. Inevitably, the scholar contemplating a public lecture had to solve the vexing problem of how to develop and express critical and creative ideas in a manner that would be compelling and novel to fellow scholars and yet clear and memorable to the young or to the nonspecialist. The difficulty of their task was compounded by the knowledge that a lecture that achieved both these ends and delighted all its listeners would have to pass equally well the critical scrutiny reserved for the printed page.

The reader of this volume may judge for himself how admirably the several contributors have succeeded in speaking to all their audiences. Unconfined by a common theme, they have lavishly displayed the riches of their imagination as of their critical art. Together, the Tupper essays make up a chapter of unusual and abiding interest in the contemporary history of Shakespeare criticism. More than that, they are a contribution to the social, philosophical, and aesthetic history of our time. For, as we all know, each generation of Shakespeare scholars makes its unique mark in large measure by what its reinterpretation of Shakespeare—his art, his ideas, and his society—reveals about the contemporary critics' own world.

*

The inaugural lecture, "Shakespeare and the Professions," by Professor Alfred Harbage of Harvard, provides wise insights into the teasing question of Shakespeare's knowledge: how could the poet have convinced members of every art, profession, and trade that he deserved to be ranked as a master of each?

Professor Arthur R. Humphreys, of the University of Leicester, combines in his "Style and Expression in *Hamlet*" an exquisitely searching stylistic analysis of the play with a closely argued rhetorical study.

Professor Madeleine Doran, of the University of Wisconsin, in her "Command, Question, and Assertion in *King Lear*," explores Shakespeare's rhetorical resources in relation to the dramatic structure of the play.

Professor Maynard Mack of Yale undertakes in *"Antony and Cleopatra*: The Stillness and the Dance" a lyrical and dramatic inquiry into the play that he calls "the delight of audiences and the despair of critics."

In "Shakespeare's Careless Art" Professor T. J. B. Spencer, director of the Shakespeare Institute and professor of English literature at the University of Birmingham, points to a diversity of ways—aesthetic, moral, and rhetorical—in which Shakespeare achieves astonishing imaginative riches of lyric and dramatic effect.

Professor James G. McManaway of the University of Maryland considers, in his "All's Well with Lafew," the central problem of defining Shakespeare's technique of bringing to life his minor as well as his major characters.

Professor Clifford Leech, of University College, the University of Toronto, develops the provocative subject "The Invulnerability of Evil," arguing that tragedy confronts us with a paradox: that only by the loss of the life of so good a man as Hamlet can evil be destroyed.

MILTON CRANE

Shakespeare and the Professions 1
ALFRED HARBAGE

The modest plan of this lecture, opening a series designed to honor a distinguished teacher, is to present some general observations about Shakespeare's knowledge of the learned professions and, more particularly, about his attitude toward professional men. Soldiers, statesmen, and monarchs stand in the foreground of most of his canvases, and about them cluster scores of attendant lords. For the moment I shall ask you to turn your eyes from these, and observe a few figures in the background or on the edges of the scene. Even these few have given rise to considerable speculation in the vast reaches of Shakespearean commentary. My familiarity with it is far from complete, but the sampling I have done has led to certain conclusions, fortified by the return which we must constantly make to Shakespeare's works themselves.

As everyone must know, lovers of Shakespeare love to claim him as their own, and tend to see in the mirror of his works, if not themselves, at least those things to which their loyalties attach. So far as I have been able to determine, the first attempt to claim Shakespeare for a profession other than the obvious one of actor and playwright came in 1790 in the Malone edition of the *Works*. Edmond Malone was a true scholar and an honest man, but he happened also to be a lawyer. It is not surprising that he concluded that the abundance of legal terms woven into the texture of the language of the plays has too great an "appearance of technical skill" to have come from a mere amateur. "I suspect," said Malone, "he was early initiated in at least the forms of law; and was employed while he yet remained at Stratford, in the office of

11

some country attorney."[1] A lengthy footnote quotes a number of legal terms used with professional accuracy, and thus
selectively assembled they seem to provide evidence of formal
training. Once the case for such training had been stated, the
supporting proof seemed to grow miraculously. In 1858 the
first full-length book on Shakespeare's legal attainments was
published. Its author, William L. Rushton, who happened also
to be a lawyer, was convinced that Shakespeare was formally
trained, and although his work is not dogmatic in tone, he
incautiously titled it *Shakespeare a Lawyer.* [2]

We can imagine how a book of this kind would strike a man
like Charles Dickens. Himself only slightly indebted to formal
education, he knew that the creative artist absorbs information
from the surrounding air, and can write on the case of Jarndyce and Jarndyce (or Shylock versus Antonio) without having qualified for the bar. In a fall issue of his magazine, *Household Words*, appears a takeoff of lawyer Rushton's book.[3]
Hydropathy was much in vogue at the time, and posing as a
hydropathist or "water-doctor," the writer claims Shakespeare
as a member of his profession. "I need hardly tell you," he
writes solemnly, "that in the very first play in our friend's
works, *The Tempest*, is the story of a great water-cure worked
in an exceedingly hard case by one Prospero." He goes on to
speak of the salutary effects of a mere dream of water upon
Clarence in *Richard III*, and of the rain therapy in *King Lear*,
especially as the old king lay in the leaky hovel. "Compare
this," he continues, "with Shakespeare's perception of mal-
practice in another case of madness, that of Ophelia, who
instead of receiving a trickle on the head, died of complete
submersion. 'Too much of water hadst thou, poor Ophelia.'
Even I myself could not have drawn the distinction with more
accuracy."

No one seemed perturbed by this offstage laughter, and in
the very next year John Campbell, who was not only a lawyer
but the Lord Chancellor of the realm, published a book on

1. *The Plays and Poems of William Shakespeare,* ed. Edmond
Malone, 10 vols. (London, 1790), 1:307.
    2. William L. Rushton, *Shakespeare a Lawyer* (London, 1858).
    3. *Household Words*, ed. Charles Dickens (23 October 1858), pp.
454-56.

Shakespeare's "legal acquirements."[4] With a lordly disregard both of Dickens's plebeian journal and Rushton's recent book, Campbell marshaled the evidence once more. Although he refrained from passing a final verdict, the effect of his argument was to tighten the claim of the lawyers upon the poet. But the competitive instinct of a rival profession was now aroused. In 1860 appeared a book called *The Medical Knowledge of Shakespeare*, which takes respectful issue with Lord Campbell and his views. The author, an actual allopath, takes a less aggressive line than the fictitious hydropath of *Household Words*, but he firmly denies that Shakespeare's knowledge of medicine was only "casual" as compared to his knowledge of law. Shakespeare, says this good Dr. Bucknill, was "a diligent student of all medical knowledge existing in his time." He refrains from claiming for the poet a "formal connection" with the medical profession because of the difficulty of visualizing him in youth as "both a lawyer's clerk and a doctor's apprentice."[5]

Thus far the discussion, although a little absurd, had been moderate and even informative. Some of the subsequent discussion has remained that way, but by no means all. Scores of books and articles have appeared, demonstrating Shakespeare's competence not only in common law but in statutory law, property law, canon law, and various more recondite branches. The Baconians soon fastened on the subject and claimed that England's Lord Chief Justice alone could have possessed such vast and expert knowledge, whereupon the defenders of Shakespeare's rights discovered that his legal knowledge was less vast and expert than they had at first supposed.[6] Much of the law in the plays, they pointed out, is "bad law." This brought rejoinders, not only from Baconians, that what might seem "bad law" to the dull eye of the common attorney could be discerned as "good law" by the bright eye of the true legal

4. John Lord Campbell, *Shakespeare's Legal Acquirements Considered* (London, 1859).

5. John C. Bucknill, *The Medical Knowledge of Shakespeare* (London, 1860), p.290.

6. F. E. Schelling points out that Sidney Lee changed his opinion about Shakespeare's legal knowledge in the revision of his biography; cf. F. E. Schelling, *Shakespeare and Demi-Science* (Philadelphia, 1927), pp. 127-28.

scholar. One need only sample this deluge of publication to learn that any kind of law has been "good law" in some time or place. With the whole world to choose from, Shakespeare could not go wrong.

Spokesmen for the medical profession have proved equally diligent. By 1873 a book had appeared on Shakespeare as a physician,[7] and scores of books and articles have followed, with titles ranging from *William Shakespeare M.D.* to "William Shakespeare, Syphilographer,"[8] demonstrating the poet's fine qualifications both as general practitioner and as specialist. We learn that the withering of Richard III's arm may have been self-induced by a strawberry, and that Macbeth's symptoms were those of battle fatigue. The mere word "itch" in the lines has proved enough to excite the dermatologist, even though the itches of our ancestors were often produced by agents which the merest layman might identify. There are treatises on Shakespeare and gynecology, obstetrics, pediatrics, ophthalmology, toxicology, pharmacology, anatomy, surgery, sanitation, and so on. There are two separate articles on "Shakespeare and the Ears, Nose, and Throat." All this sounds more ludicrous than it really is. Most of this printed matter appears in medical journals, with the innocent intention of sweetening the clinical air with a few quotations from the beloved poet. There is something engaging about the eagerness of the authors to have Shakespeare share their own intense interest in scabies, twinning, "laterality dominance," and the like.The physicians must be praised for their restraint, never having claimed that their revered Renaissance predecessor, Dr. William Harvey, was the true author of the plays even though the characters seem to have circulating blood.

We may ask what the teaching profession has been doing about drawing Shakespeare into its orbit, and must answer that its members have been strangely negligent, particularly so

7. H. Aubert, *Shakespeare als Mediziner* (Rostak, 1873).

8. H. B. Epstein, *William Shakespeare, M. D.* (Newark, 1932); W. E. Vest, "William Shakespeare, Syphilographer," *West Virginia Medical Journal* 34 (1938): 130-37. (I have not consulted these works.) For the recent writings on Shakespeare's medical knowledge, see G. R. Smith, *A Classified Shakespeare Bibliography, 1936-1958* (University Park, Pa., 1963), pp. 98-99. More prodigious both in amount and content are the writings by the psychoanalysts; see ibid., pp. 47-56.

since teaching is the sole vocation outside the theater with which Shakespeare can be associated on documentary grounds. John Aubrey, the seventeenth-century recorder of miscellaneous information, was told by the son of one of Shakespeare's fellow actors, Christopher Beeston, that the poet was "in his younger yeares a School-master in the Countrey."[9] Unlike the legends about deer poaching and the like, this report has a clear and good descent; and since it is not picturesque, exciting, or scandalous, there would have been small point in preserving it except for the fact that it was true. If a mere eighteenth-century guess that he had served a legal apprenticeship could translate Shakespeare into a lawyer, we may well wonder why a good seventeenth-century record that he served a teaching apprenticeship has not translated him into a fellow of Oxford or Cambridge. Certainly his works teem with supporting evidence. Every line displays his proficiency in the chief subject of the Renaissance curriculum, the art of communication.[10] He could have given advanced courses in declamation, rhetoric, and literature; and since he was the coiner of the words "critic" and "critical," we can even guess at his approach. Still there have been no books called "Professor William Shakespeare" or "William Shakespeare, Ph.D.," and we can only conclude that teachers are an unacquisitive or listless race.

Before drawing any conclusions about Shakespeare's competence in the learned professions, we should recognize that the ease with which he exploited their language is part of a general phenomenon. The competing books about Shakespeare as a sailor, a soldier, and so on should serve as sufficient reminder. Perhaps the most convincing book of all would present Shakespeare as a gamekeeper, since he shows an uncanny familiarity with the sports of field and forest. Nevertheless, it is true that we are constantly struck by surprising items of information—legal, medical, linguistic—subtending the imagery

9. John Aubrey, *Brief Lives*; cf. E. K. Chambers, *William Shakespeare*, 2 vols. (Oxford, 1930), 2:254.

10. A book by J. P. Chesney, *Shakespeare as a Physician* (St. Louis, 1884), is organized like a medical textbook. One may compare with it a book not designed to prove Shakespeare a teacher of rhetoric, and yet approximating a manual on the subject: Sister Miriam Joseph, *Shakespeare's Use of the Arts of Language* (New York, 1947).

of the plays. It is usually not of the kind that would be "looked up" for the particular occasion, since the occasion is often inappropriate. It is too often forgotten that Shakespeare's plays, although written in Elizabethan England, were not set in Elizabethan England. In nineteen of them the scene is the coastal lands and islands of the Mediterranean, often in ancient times. In one it is medieval Denmark, in one a decadent Vienna, in three a dateless France. The remaining fourteen are indeed set in the British Isles, but in times ancient, medieval, or early Tudor. We make an exception of *The Merry Wives of Windsor*, even though Falstaff, its principal character, seems to have died on the eve of Agincourt in 1415, since, except for this detail, the setting is indubitably English and contemporary. But in all of the rest of the plays set in England the most "modern" episode is the birth of Queen Elizabeth, which occurred thirty years before Shakespeare himself was born. Under the circumstances any material in these plays reflecting *Elizabethan* life and learning is there in the form of seepage. It is not only incidental, but also inadvertent and anachronistic. Logically, it should not be there at all.

But, of course, it *is* there; and what this seems to mean is that Shakespeare was attuned to his environment. He responded to the life of his times sensitively and with relish. The human mind retains best those things which interest it most, and the astonishing retentiveness of Shakespeare's mind is the gauge of the width of his interests. It was a curiously extroverted mind, compared with those of the more seriously regarded writers of our own day, many of whom seem able to think of nothing except thinking and to write of nothing except writing. So far as the professions are concerned, I believe that we can come to one sound conclusion. The wealth of informed imagery and allusion relating to them does not prove that Shakespeare was formally trained in all or any one of them, but it does prove that he was just as much interested in professional activity as in political and martial activity. One would not have guessed this from his choice of story material—dictated, of course, by its theatrical viability as well as its interest to him personally—and so the discussions of his "knowledge," however eccentric at times, have not really been in vain.

The question which naturally follows is whether Shakespeare's interest in the professions was attended by respect. What did he think of the value of professional activity, and of the character of professional men? A word of caution is necessary at this point. A character in a play is bound to take on the coloration of the context, and to be shaped in conformity with the principle of decorum. Thus, in Shakespeare's time, it was less permissible to create a clownish king or general than to create a clownish doctor or teacher, and also less likely that commanding figures would figure in farcical plays. A teacher or doctor in a farce may well appear as a farcical teacher or doctor, whereas in a tragedy he would not have done so. We cannot determine from Shakespeare's comical or serious treatment of individual professional men just how seriously he regarded the professions they represent. Rather we must observe the limits he set upon the ridicule in the ridiculous portraits, and what form the seriousness took in the serious portraits. Only then may we penetrate to his underlying attitudes. What we discover is that Shakespeare's instinct was to set a limit to ridicule, and to respect what he apparently deemed to be the most fundamental tenet of each professional code.

I may illustrate the point by speaking briefly of his portraits of members of the working clergy. Technically, no Protestants should appear in the plays at all since the time and place of action is invariably Catholic when it is not pagan, but a scattering of parsons appear, and even a few Puritans. These may receive comic treatment, but unlike similar clergymen in the plays of Jonson and Middleton, they are never lampooned as frauds. Great fun is made of Nathaniel in *Love's Labor's Lost*, but this "foolish mild man" is finally described both as "honest" and "a marvellous good neighbor."[11] We catch only a glimpse of Oliver Martext in *As You Like It*. His name must be a jibe at the Puritans, but he is not divested of dignity. After his rebuff by Jaques and Touchstone he lifts his chin stoutly: " 'Tis no matter. Ne'er a fantastical knave of them all shall flout me out of my calling."[12] This kind of qualifying

11. *Love's Labor's Lost,* V, ii, 575-77. All plays are cited in the *Complete Pelican Shakespeare,* ed. Alfred Harbage (Baltimore: Penguin Books Inc., 1956-67; collected ed., 1969).
12. *As You Like It,* III, iii, 93-94.

touch is apt to be puzzling to the modern reader; and, of course, in the more heavy-handed kind of stage production, it is always crudely eradicated. When Malvolio, in far-off and Catholic Illyria, is called "a kind of Puritan," a distinction immediately follows: "The devil a Puritan that he is, or anything constantly but a time-pleaser."[13] By implication the Puritans, however lacking in geniality or bad for theatrical business, must be regarded as at least sincere. Jonson and Middleton never blurred their comic stereotypes with admissions so damaging.

Or consider Shakespeare's friars. Five appear in the plays: Laurence and John in *Romeo and Juliet*, Francis in *Much Ado About Nothing*, and Peter and Thomas in *Measure for Measure*. Three of them have New Testament names, all seem to wear "cowls" and to dwell in appropriate "cells" or religious "houses," but there the verisimilitude ends. These are most fictitious friars: it would be hard from the data supplied in the plays to deduce the rule or even the function of the Franciscan or other mendicant orders. In fact their chief function as here suggested is to dream up unlikely intrigues or to run errands in those dreamed up by others. But along with the general impression that friars live a clandestine life on the fringes of society, another is also conveyed—that friars are mild, kindly, and truly religious men. Now in the London where Shakespeare wrote, the former frater-hall of the Dominicans was serving as a commercial playhouse, and this was considered by most Londoners as a distinct improvement over its former sinister use. Why then are Shakespeare's Laurence, John, Peter, Francis, and Thomas such "nice" men—much "nicer" really than the friars of Chaucer, whose London teemed with their kind? We may say that distance has lent enchantment, but this was not so in Elizabethan drama generally. Libelous representation of the old religious orders was common if not universal. It is conspicuous, for instance, in *The Troublesome Reign of King John*; and it is characteristic of Shakespeare that, when he came to rework this play, he expunged the scenes displaying corruption among the rank and file of the church although he granted no similar immunity to its upper hierarchical fig-

13. *Twelfth Night*, II, iii, 134-35.

ures. All ties together to give us a reliable impression of a Shakespearean attitude. He could treat the working clergy as sometimes futile or comic, but he was disinclined to treat them, whether Catholic or Protestant, as vicious, corrupt, or negligent in their office. He seems to have felt that the one thing that a professed man of God must not be is hypocritical.

In the case of teachers, I should guess that the unpardonable fault in Shakespeare's eyes was indifference. Pedantry in a teacher, or even aspiring ignorance, might be treated as laughable, but not a contempt for learning. It has been said that schoolmasters were the one class of men whom he could not bring himself to like,[14] but the evidence does not really sustain this judgment. It is true that schoolmasters are alluded to by his characters as impoverished and despised, as they were in fact in Elizabethan times (and often since), and it is also true that going to school is mentioned with distaste. We hear of

> the whining schoolboy, with his satchel
> And shining morning face, creeping like snail
> Unwillingly to school.

(As You Like It, II, vii, 145-47)

and this is by no means the only passage evoking the idea of school-going as durance vile. But we must remember that even the progressive movement has failed to plant in the human heart an abiding love of school, and that the Elizabethan schools were not progressive. They were places where Latin grammar was instilled by means of rote recitation and the rod in sessions of eight hours a day, six days a week, all months of the year. Unlike the patients of the doctors, whose methods were equally rigorous, the pupils of the schoolmasters survived to tell the tale, and it would have been impossible for Shakespeare to refer to the school memories of his audience as anything but traumatic.

The fact that the schoolmasters who appear in his plays are comic figures relates, of course, to the fact that they appear in farces. Under the circumstances it is remarkable that they do not appear as ogres—are not portrayed as cruel or cynical.

14. J. Dover Wilson, "The Schoolmaster in Shakespeare's Plays," *Essays by Divers Hands being the Transactions of the Royal Society of Literature of the United Kingdom*, ed. J. Bailey, n.s., 9 (Oxford, 1930): 9-34.

Even the lamentable Pinch in *The Comedy of Errors*, described as a "pedant and a conjuror" (because of his command of Latin) is a dutiful man according to his lights. The lampoon of Holofernes in *Love's Labor's Lost* is hilariously funny precisely because of this schoolmaster's sublime sense of mission and absorption in his subject. He sees people as parts of speech: "A soul feminine saluteth us,"[15] he observes of Jaquenetta's greeting; and he thinks of rank in terms of phonetics: "thou consonant,"[16] he calls little Moth, because consonants without vowels are nothing. He is a supercilious ass—there is no question of that—but he is also outgiving, and his pedantical ardor is winning. One would prefer to send one's child to Holofernes's charge-house on the top of the mountain than to Squeers's Dotheboys Hall, or even to more reputable schools one might name. What he learned would be somewhat strange, a bit on the precious side, but he would at least learn something, and might even be ignited by Holofernes's synthetic sparks.

Hugh Evans in *The Merry Wives of Windsor*, teaching Latin with a Welsh accent, is an appealing figure, timorously brave and full of moral feeling. He is the one Shakespearean schoolmaster whom we actually see teaching.[17] He uses a judicious mixture of threat and encouragement as he hears little William's declensions: "hig, hag, hog . . . horum, harum, horum." When Mistress Quickly protests that the child should not be exposed to such nasty words as "horum" or, indeed, to the genitive case at all, master Evans speaks for all poor teachers who have been harassed by unqualified censors: "For shame, 'oman . . . art thou lunatics!" He threatens William with the rod when he trips on "qui, quae, quod," but what he actually does is to send him off to share in a recess: "Go your ways and play, go."

Elizabethan law courts, like grammar schools, were not calculated to leave fragrant memories and evoke images of delight. Shakespeare's high regard for Law, spelled with a capital letter, is a commonplace of commentary; but its day-to-day proceedings and practitioners must have seemed to him, as to

15. *Love's Labor's Lost*, IV, ii, 77.
16. *Ibid*, V, i, 49.
17. *Merry Wives of Windsor*, IV, i.

everyone else, less lovely and majestic than the cause they presumably served. Hamlet laments the "law's delay" and alludes to the lawyer's "tricks" and "quiddities."[18] Jaques speaks of the lawyer's peculiar aberration as "politic"[19] (meaning in this context "devious"), and when Queen Mab's tiny train passes over the fingers of the sleeping lawyer, he dreams of "fees."[20] In a word, the language of the plays often reflects those irritations which are a feature of universal experience. But this kind of reference is not overabundant, and our general impression is that Shakespeare viewed the legal processes, so ubiquitous in his life and times, without illusion but also without disgust. They had to be lived with, like the rain which raineth every day.

When we try to appraise his attitude to members of the profession, we are met by a curiosity. Court scenes and legalistic entanglements abound in the plays, but there are no practicing attorneys. Among Shakespeare's more than seven hundred characters only one is explicitly tagged as lawyer, an almost invisible character in *1 Henry VI*. We never see a lawyer consulting with a client, transacting his business, or pleading his case. Even Shylock, who sorely needs one, appears in court without a lawyer. Portia posing as Dr. Bellario is the nearest we come to a portrait of a member of the profession in action. Her success in court (if not her indifference to a monetary fee) must be credited in part to the absent Paduan; his were the acute legal brains and hers the eloquence. In the hearing of Brabantio versus Othello, each of the principals pleads his own case, and this is entirely typical: we think of the "trial" of Hermione in *The Winter's Tale*, and of the several "trials" in *Measure for Measure*. Perhaps Shakespeare, with his own matchless qualifications to practice, excluded rival lawyers as superfluous.

On the other hand, there are judges and justices—some of them ex officio, like the several presiding dukes, others by virtue of their formal preparation. The latter vary in type from the Lord Chief Justice who is Falstaff's nemesis, to Justice Shallow, whom Falstaff mulcts. Justice Shallow has studied

18. *Hamlet*, III, i, 72; V, i, 92-93.
19. *As You Like It*, IV, i, 13.
20. *Romeo and Juliet*, I, iv, 73.

law at Lincoln's Inn and knows that "A friend i' th' court is better than a penny in purse," but it is his servingman Davy who applies the principle—on behalf of his friend Visor: "I grant your worship that he is a knave, sir, but yet God forbid, sir, but a knave should have some countenance at his friend's request. An honest man, sir, is able to speak for himself."[21] This seems reasonable to Justice Shallow, but even his dim light keeps the laws of the realm faintly legible: he tries to administer the impressment act honestly and to send the King the best recruits. Shakespeare's justices, and even his constables, like Dogberry, try to use good judgment, although not with complete success, and his judges try to be just. The unjust judge Angelo in *Measure for Measure* is the exception that proves the rule; and he is counterpoised by the just judge Escalus, whose patience and fairness are exemplary as he copes with the vice of a demoralized Vienna.

It is apparent that Shakespeare was reluctant to show members of the legal professions as perverters of the law, using it as mere instrument of gain or aggression. The fact that he portrays no practicing lawyers at all may seem to reduce the significance of the fact that he portrays no shysters. On the other hand, the opportunity was there and a number of his contemporaries seized it. Their freedom underscores his restraint. Lawyers in claiming Shakespeare as their own have been willing to forgive his failure to give members of their profession work. The practice of the law is more generously treated by him than by almost any other major English writer.

The medical profession has even more reason to feel grateful. Except in Shakespeare, the portrait of the doctor in Elizabethan drama is prevailingly hostile. Even the tolerant Thomas Dekker called medicine the "Ars Homicidiorum"[22] and viewed its practitioners as a menace. He was not far wrong. With its leechings, cuppings, bleedings, and violent purgings, and its armament of fantastic potions, medical practice at the time was an ally of disease. An energetic and conscientious lawyer was then as useful to a client in trouble as at any time before or since, but the more energetic and conscientious the doctor, the greater the danger to the patient. One's

21. *Henry IV,* V, i, 27-28, 37-40.
22. Thomas Dekker, *The Guls Hornbook.*

chance of recovery was greater, then and for some generations to come, if he could not afford a doctor. It is a matter of peculiar interest, therefore, that Shakespeare's doctors, unlike those of fact and fiction in his times, are shown not only as exemplary in their personal characters, but as successful in working cures.

It has been suggested that Shakespeare's apparent esteem for the profession stems from his esteem for his son-in-law, Dr. John Hall, and the possibility is worth a glance. The earlier plays portray only one physician, the fiery Frenchman Caius, who in *The Merry Wives of Windsor* is the mother's unsuccessful candidate for the hand of "sweet Ann Page." We do not see Dr. Caius practicing medicine, but only displaying his comical ineligibility as a bridegroom. Dr. Hall almost certainly arrived in Stratford after Shakespeare had written his village farce, and unlike Dr. Caius, he must have seemed eligible indeed for the hand of any unattached maiden. He was a gentleman born, a man of substance, a graduate of Cambridge, and a licentiate of the College of Physicians, destined to win a fine reputation both for piety and for devotion to his work. He was thirty-two, eleven years younger than his father-in-law, when his marriage to Susanna Shakespeare occurred in June 1607. Susanna was then twenty-four, and already a spinster by the standards of the day. A daughter, Elizabeth, born to the couple in 1608, was Shakespeare's only grandchild at the time of his death, and his will reveals how his hopes for a lasting posterity were linked to this little girl. We must concede that there is good reason to suppose that he felt esteem and even gratitude to Dr. John Hall. His flattering portraits of doctors occur in plays written from 1602 onwards, some of them certainly and all of them possibly after he had come to know this admirable man. The fact may be significant or it may be a mere coincidence. There is a distinct possibility that the doctors in his *dramatis personae* would have appeared pretty much as they are had the playwright had no acquaintance or family connection with a member of the medical profession, since his attitude toward it is no different in essentials from his attitude toward the professions in general.

In *All's Well That Ends Well* we hear of Dr. Gerard de Narbon, "whose skill was almost as great as his honesty; had it stretched so far, would have made nature immortal."[23] The King of France remembers him as a paragon, and one of his remedies, posthumously administered by his daughter Helena, saves the King's life. In *Pericles* the physician Cerimon is thus addressed:

Your honor has through Ephesus poured forth
Your charity, and hundreds call themselves
Your creatures, who by you have been restored;
And not your knowledge, your personal pain, but even
Your purse, still open, hath built Lord Cerimon
Such strong renown as time shall never raze.

(Pericles, III, ii, 42-47)

In snatching Thaisa from death when her cold body is tossed upon the shores of Ephesus, Cerimon administers one of his "blest infusions." Like Narbon's lifesaving remedy, it remains tactfully undescribed, but we can surely approve of the rest of the treatment—warmth, dry linens, and aftercare: "And Aesculapius guide us!" In *Cymbeline* the physician Cornelius thwarts the murderous Queen by supplying her only an opiate when she asks for poison. Cornelius protests even against her pretext for wanting the latter, that is to conduct experiments on animals:

Your Highness
Shall from this practice but make hard your heart.

(Cymbeline, I, v, 23-24)

Even more impressive are the physicians in *King Lear* and *Macbeth*. In preparing to treat the frenzy of Lear, the nameless doctor says,

Our foster nurse of nature is repose,
The which he lacks. That to provoke in him
Are many simples operative, whose power
Will close the eye of anguish

(King Lear, IV, iv, 12-15)

He prescribes nothing further than a sedative, fresh garments, music, and, wisest remedy of all, the attendance of Cordelia at his side. The treatment deserved its success. Dr. Hall's casebook has recently been edited, and we are able to satisfy our curiosity about what Shakespeare's son-in-law might have prescribed in a similar situation. Although not called

23. *All's Well That Ends Well*, I, i, 17-18.

upon to treat King Lear, aged fourscore and upwards, he
was called upon to treat one Master Kempson, aged threescore
and "oppressed with Melancholy, and a Feaver with extraordinary heat."[24] He applied to the soles of the patient's feet
"Radishes sliced besprinkled with Vinegar and Salt" to draw
back the "Vapours" which caused "starting and fear." This
was his mildest prescription. Leeches were applied, and
enemas, physics, and emetics administered, all composed of
frightening ingredients. We are reminded of lines in the non-
Shakespearean part of *Pericles*:

Thou speak'st like a physician, Helicanus,
That ministers a potion unto me
That thou would'st tremble to receive thyself.

(Pericles, I, ii, 66-68)

One of these potions was an "Emetick Infusion" containing
"oxymel of Squils," which produced, as the casebook faithfully records, "four Vomits and nine Stools." Master Kempson
recovered and, as Dr. Hall happily notes, "lived for many
years." It was, as he says and as we can agree, "beyond all
expectation."

In *Macbeth*, the doctor is called upon to treat perturbations
less violent than Lear's but also less remediable. He detects a
sickness of the soul, and says, "This disease is beyond my
practice." [25] We owe to Professor Kocher the note that this
doctor's dilemma reflects an Elizabethan controversy.[26] Physicians were suspected of being atheistic empirics, inclined to
believe that even the pricks of conscience could be treated as
physical symptoms. It was a prophetic issue: our psychiatric
science has not yet defined for us the precise boundary between sick sense of guilt and wholesome sense of guiltiness,
and how we can cure the one without killing the other.
Shakespeare's doctor is religiously orthodox when he refrains
from prescribing for Lady Macbeth: "More needs she the
divine than the physician." He is consistent when addressed by
Macbeth:

24. Harriet Joseph, *Shakespeare's Son-in-law: John Hall, Man and
Physician* (Hamden, Conn., 1964), pp. 26-27.
25. *Macbeth*, V, i, 54.
26. Paul Kocher, "Lady Macbeth and the Doctor," *Shakespeare
Quarterly* 5 (1954): 341-49.

Canst thou not minister to a mind diseased,
Pluck from the memory a rooted sorrow,
Raze out the written troubles of the brain,
And with some sweet oblivious antidote
(Macbeth, V, Cleanse the stuffed bosom of that perilous stuff
iii, 40-45) Which weighs upon the heart?

This sounds wonderfully modern, like a description of
neurotic symptoms, but the doctor responds as to a confession: "Therein the patient must minister to himself."
    Nevertheless, this Scotch practitioner resembles in an impor-
tant particular the Briton who treats the more sinned against
than sinning Lear. He is solicitous for the welfare of Lady
Macbeth, even though horrified by his guess at the cause of her
condition. He feels no impulse to expose her, and does all that
he can do:

God, God, forgive us all! Look after her;
(Macbeth, V, Remove from her the means of all annoyance,
i, 70-72) And still keep eyes upon her.

True, he would like to be far from Dunsinane—"Profit again
should hardly draw me here"—but while there in attendance,
he remains true to his professional as well as his religious code.
    If we omit the word "learned" and accept as "professional"
all those nonmenial occupations in which members of the middle class serve society, we find that the group so occupied in
Shakespeare's plays—the shipmasters, stewards, women-in-
waiting, prison officials, and the like—yields his highest per-
centage of decent characters, unheroic though they may be.
Surprisingly enough, Shakespeare's jailers are as conscientious
and humane as his physicians, and the steward Flavius is the
one truly fine character in the play where he appears. We may
question, I think, the common assumption that Shakespeare's
social bias was aristocratic, but that is scarcely the point.
Whatever his social bias, the idea of human service on the
nonspectacular plane held considerable appeal to him. And he
was averse to attacking institutions, even those so vulnerable as
the College of Physicians. Since its future was bright although
its present was gloomy, we can scarcely complain that he viewed
it in terms of its ideals rather than its accomplishments. He

served the long-range truth better than did the satiric realists, although the latter stuck closer to the facts.

I should like to conclude with mention of a somewhat more imposing representative of Professor Tupper's profession, and my own, than Holofernes and Hugh Evans. When I was honored with the invitation to give this lecture, the accompanying tribute to Professor Tupper described him as a "man of quiet dignity who combined an avid enthusiasm for literature with an active interest in the world about him." Upon asking myself to what character in Shakespeare these words would best apply, the answer came at once—to Prospero in *The Tempest*. Prospero's "avid enthusiasm for literature" lost him his dukedom. The "liberal arts," he says, were "all my study" and "my library/Was dukedom large enough."[27] But when exiled to his island, he left his ivory tower. He still had his beloved books, and he now applied them in his "active interest in the world about him." Although there were only two youngsters on the island, Caliban and Miranda, he promptly opened a school. Since he himself describes himself as "schoolmaster," teachers, I think, have as much right to claim him for their profession as the physicians have to claim Cerimon, who was also a lordly amateur.

Prospero's score as teacher was one failure and one success. The dropout Caliban snarls at his old master: "You taught me language, and my profit on't/Is, I know how to curse."[28] It is a frightening utterance, not without present-day relevance. Neither is Caliban's morose and pathetic conception of "freedom," freedom to be bestial rather than human. But Prospero's graduate, Miranda, justifies his pedagogical pride:

> ... here
> Have I, thy schoolmaster, made thee more profit
> Than other princess can, that had more time
> For vainer hours, and tutors not so careful.

(The Tempest, I, ii, 171-74)

Miranda is both cultivated and full of hope:

> How beauteous mankind is! O brave new world
> That has such people in 't!

(The Tempest, V, i, 183-84)

27. *The Tempest*, I, ii, 73-74, 109-10.
28. *Ibid.*, I, ii, 363-64.

This, too, is not without present-day relevance. Miranda is the idealistic graduate who, by thinking the world better than it is, may help to make it so. A teacher who produces one Miranda may consider his career a success. I am sure that Professor Tupper's score was better than that. This lecture series stands as evidence that he was able to create gratitude, one of the most precious virtues.

Finally I should like to say that Shakespeare's teaching career was a success. It is unfashionable to speak of literary art as a form of teaching, but it can be so in one of its effects. The members of all professions like to think of Shakespeare as their own because he expressed their aspirations. All who profess humanity have learned something in Shakespeare's school.

Style and Expression in *Hamlet*

ARTHUR R. HUMPHREYS

2

Whichever of Shakespeare's greater plays one is reading is apt to seem, at that moment, the finest of all. Yet powerful though the magnetism is of *Romeo and Juliet* or *Henry IV* or *Othello* or *King Lear* or *The Winter's Tale*, surely it is *Hamlet* which exerts the supreme spell. Its supremacy in popular esteem is a function of its inexhaustible mysteriousness, a function also of the unrivaled wealth of invention and stimulus which makes hungry the appetite where most it satisfies. "Simply as a play of things happening," Dr. Tillyard observes, "of one event being bred out of another, and of each event being described with appropriate and unwearied brilliance, *Hamlet* is supreme."[1] Yet such supremacy depends on its supremacy as poetry. John Masefield once remarked that the play confronts us everywhere, every day, except in the theater.[2] Things are better now—or are they? However that may be, the remark at least recognizes how wide is the fascination of its haunting and marvelous words.

The words I propose to discuss are principally those in the verse, though in a real sense "poetic style" is not a verse monopoly. Much of *Hamlet* is in prose, and even the Prince himself, after he has encountered the Ghost, speaks mainly prose save when he soliloquizes or talks with Horatio; he addresses the King so, and the court and Ophelia and the players. The

Shakespeare quotations are from the Cambridge edition of *Hamlet*, ed. John Dover Wilson (Cambridge: Cambridge University Press, 1934).

1. E. M. W. Tillyard, *Shakespeare's Problem Plays* (Toronto: University of Toronto Press, 1950), p. 26.

2. John Masefield, *William Shakespeare* (New York: H. Holt & Co., 1912), p. 167.

great closet scene with Gertrude is in verse, however, since
here he drops any easy familiarity or any mask of distraction.
A. E. Housman held that no thought or feeling, however subtle
or elevated, was too good to be couched in prose;[3] and when
one recalls Hamlet's address to Rosencrantz and Guildenstern
on "this goodly frame, the earth, . . . this most excellent cano-
py the air, . . . this brave o'erhanging firmament, this majestical roof fretted with golden fire" (II, ii, 302-5) one is disposed
to agree. My reasons for bypassing the prose are two. One is
that the verse itself offers more than enough for my theme and
time. The other is that the very passage I have quoted is dis-
cussed in Dr. Milton Crane's study entitled *Shakespeare's Prose*
(Chicago: University of Chicago Press, 1951), and Dr. Crane
treats the prose of *Hamlet* so well as to leave me nothing to
do. So let me attend to the verse, and let us, as C. S. Lewis
counseled us to do, "surrender [ourselves] to the poetry and
the situation."[4]

For Dr. Johnson (see his notes on the play), *Hamlet's* distinguishing excellence was its variety. Levin Schücking, re-
fining on the same perception, discerns in it "a truly baroque
exuberance."[5] It explores all the things Shakespeare had prac-
ticed making verse do, in expressive imagery, responsive texture and rhythm, and verbal equivalence to swift and complex
thought and feeling. Hamlet's own utterance, Dame Rebecca
West has written,

runs with the quick, ranging gait of thought, of the interior
monologue, and as we listen to it we recognise that that is how
we think. . . . Hamlet speaks with a quick, springing harmony
recognisable as the voice of physical and mental splendour; his
mind travels like lightning, yet strikes below the surface.[6]

A style so defined is a metaphor for the whole play. Here
Shakespeare most fully achieves what, in Coleridge's opinion,
poetry should give:

3. A. E. Housman, *The Name and Nature of Poetry* (New York:
Macmillan, 1933), p. 36.
4. C. S. Lewis, "Hamlet: The Prince or the Poem?" *Proceedings of
the British Academy* (London; H. Milford, 1942), 28:145.
5. Levin L. Schücking, *The Meaning of Hamlet* (London: Oxford
University Press, 1937), p. 46.
6. Rebecca West, *The Court and the Castle* (London: Macmillan,
1958), pp. 10, 24.

a pleasure from the whole consistent with a consciousness of pleasure from the component parts;—and the perfection of which is, to communicate from each part the greatest immediate pleasure compatible with the largest sum of pleasure on the whole.[7]

It is in *Hamlet*, above all the other plays, that consciousness of the highest local pleasure is consistent with the "largest sum of pleasure on the whole."

Here above all Shakespeare displays what Coleridge asks for:

deep feeling and exquisite sense of beauty, both as exhibited to the eye in combinations of form, and to the ear in sweet and appropriate melody.[8]

Hamlet is the play in which Shakespeare turns from the world of rich, moving, yet confident comedy to that of metaphysical tragedy, seeking to know whether man, the paragon of animals, is more than the quintessence of dust and, if he is, what are the qualities which make him so. Of this the great histories, and *Julius Caesar*, had given a foretaste, but a foretaste merely. Deep feelings now reflect themselves in complex though not tortured verse. The sense of beauty is stirred by reminders of lost goodness, recollections of an uncorrupted past. Sweet and appropriate melody sounds again and again; there is a *Hamlet* music as there is a *Twelfth Night* music, an *Othello* music, an *Antony and Cleopatra* music, individual, unmistakable, sounding in lines which balance and float and sing in the mind's ear—lines like "In equal scale weighing delight and dole" (I, ii, 13), or "Colleaguéd with this dream of his advantage" (I, ii, 21), or "Grapple them unto thy soul with hoops of steel" (I, iii, 63), or "Th'expectancy and rose of the fair state" (III, i, 155). Fluency of rhythm, haunting poise of stress, and magical modulation of vowel and consonant seem particularly the notes of this play. If indeed one cannot pass a day without reading or hearing something from *Hamlet*, the reason is the character of passages like the following, where musical polysyllables play on a groundwork of the plain and simple:

7. Samuel Taylor Coleridge, *Shakespearean Criticism*, ed. T. M. Raysor (New York: E. P. Dutton, 1960), 1:148.
8. Ibid., 1:187.

We do it wrong being so majestical
To offer it the show of violence,
For it is as the air, invulnerable,
(I, i, 143-46) And our vain blows malicious mockery.

This lithe and melodious writing differs much from the richly
rhetorical manner of *Othello* or the harshly grand manner of
Lear, but finds some analogy in the shifts and turns of brood-
ing and speculation Shakespeare gives to his other great tragic-
imaginative poet, Macbeth. Granville-Barker discusses the lines
with which Hamlet opens Gertrude's eyes to the enormity of
her fault:

Rebellious hell,
If thou canst mutine in a matron's bones,
To flaming youth let virtue be as wax
And melt in her own fire. Proclaim no shame
When the compulsive ardour gives the charge,
Since frost itself as actively doth burn,
(III, iv, 82-88) And reason pandars will.

He analyzes the rich constituents of vowels and consonants
here, and shows how the actor is offered a sound pattern in
which he can, as it were, "play over" the fascination Hamlet
himself finds in the sensuality of words. The richly expressive
texture, the swift onward drive of rhythm, the fugal dynamics
of vowels and consonants express Hamlet's thoughts in their
mercurial velocity, urged on by the compulsive ardor of his
own extravagance.[9]
    How it is that the *Hamlet* style so intimately weds sound,
sense, and passion it is hard to say, but throughout the play
the most subtle relationships are maintained between words
and meanings. Take, for instance, the following:

What art thou that usurp'st this time of night
Together with that fair and warlike form
In which the majesty of buried Denmark
(I, i, 46-49) Did sometimes march? By heaven I charge thee speak!

"Usurp'st," the verb for the outrage to night's peace and for
the seemingly lawless assuming of King Hamlet's form by the

    9. Harley Granville-Barker, *Prefaces to Shakespeare: Third Series*
(London: Sidgwick & Jackson, 1937), pp. 203–4.

ghost, is a word of intrusive and awkward sound, thrusting itself into the supple language of the line like an alien; as its sound insists on its eccentricity, so its meaning includes the wrongful ousting of good by ill, the upset of nature's order, and the dubious status of the ghost. Then the procession of modulated vowels ("time," "night," "fair," "warlike," "form"), the consonantal liaisons ("form," "majesty," "Denmark," "sometimes march"), and the melodiously grandiloquent diction imply the dignity of the true King against the shocking presence of the intruder. The whole usage of language is wonderfully alert in relating sense to pace, texture, and music.

Professor Wolfgang Clemen has remarked on "the surprisingly new possibilities of language which make this play appear a turning-point in the development of Shakespeare's style."[10] These, he observes, "seem to have their origin in the character of Hamlet." That Hamlet's character, with its vivacity, its brilliance, its complexity, should reflect itself in new possibilities of language is what Shakespeare's creative identification with his subjects would lead us to expect. The focal aspect of style may be represented by Hamlet's praise of Horatio, where a condensed metaphor characteristic of the later complex writing—the writing of *Troilus and Cressida* or *Measure for Measure* or *King Lear*—alternates with the earlier unaffected directness characteristic of *Julius Caesar*:

> Why should the poor be flattered?
> No, let the candied tongue lick absurd pomp,
> And crook the pregnant hinges of the knee
> Where thrift may follow fawning. Dost thou hear?
> Since my dear soul was mistress of her choice,
> And could of men distinguish her election,
> Sh'hath sealed thee for herself, for thou hast been
> As one in suff'ring all that suffers nothing,
> A man that Fortune's buffets and rewards
> Has ta'en with equal thanks; and blest are those
> Whose blood and judgment are so well co-medled,
> That they are not a pipe for Fortune's finger
> To sound what stop she please: give me that man

10. Wolfgang H. Clemen, *The Development of Shakespeare's Imagery* (Cambridge, Mass.: Harvard University Press, 1951), p. 106.

That is not passion's slave, and I will wear him
In my heart's core, ay in my heart of heart,
(III, ii, 57-72) As I do thee.

That is not two styles, the tricky and the clear, meeting by
accident. In the compressed, allusive dog-image ("the candied
tongue" and "pregnant hinges of the knee") Hamlet is enact-
ing his indignant wrestle with flattery and his nauseated revul-
sion from it; in his praise of Horatio he expresses the lucidity
of his mind in a situation he can trust, his clear affection for a
friend whose honor calls forth his own honesty, the man
"more an antique Roman than a Dane" who is appropriately
addressed in a style which would fit into *Julius Caesar*.

Other qualities already developed for simpler ends now
serve the new possibilities of language. The lyricism of natural
beauty and wholesomeness, besides providing its immediate
charm, has a deep and moving significance; it represents a
whole vanishing world. As the action begins, night's freezing
darkness is haunted by evil. The cock crows, the ghost departs,
and Horatio and Marcellus feel the polar contrast between its
baleful presence and the purity of Christian blessing:

Barnardo: It was about to speak when the cock crew.
Horatio: And then it started like a guilty thing,
    Upon a fearful summons; I have heard
    The cock that is trumpet to the morn
    Doth with his lofty and shrill-sounding throat
    Awake the god of day, and at his warning
    Whether in sea or fire, in earth or air,
    Th'extravagant and erring spirit hies
    To his confine, and of the truth herein
    This present object made probation.
Marcellus: It faded on the crowing of the cock.
    Some say that ever 'gainst that season comes
    Wherein our Saviour's birth is celebrated,
    This bird of dawning singeth all night long,
    And then they say no spirit dare stir abroad,
    The nights are wholesome, then no planets strike,
    No fairy takes, nor witch hath power to charm,
    So hallowed, and so gracious is that time.
Horatio: So have I heard and do in part believe it.
    But look, the morn in russet mantle clad

> Walks o'er the dew of yon high eastward hill.
> Break we our watch up.   *(I. i, 147-68)*

Alleging that *Hamlet* is "most certainly an artistic failure," T. S. Eliot objected to its variability of style—"both workmanship and thought are in an unstable position," he wrote. He offered Horatio's lines on the russet-mantled morn as evidence that the play is a mixture of earlier, immature styles (as that of *Romeo and Juliet*) and late, mature ones (as when Hamlet explains to Horatio how he foiled the King's plot against him):[11]

Hamlet: Sir, in my heart there was a kind of fighting
          That would not let me sleep—methought I lay
          Worse than the mutines in the bilboes. Rashly,
          And praised be rashness for it—let us know
          Our indiscretion sometime serves us well,
          When our deep plots do pall, and that should learn us
          There's a divinity that shapes our ends,
          Rough-hew them how we will—
Horatio: That is most certain.
Hamlet: Up from my cabin,
          My sea-gown scarfed about me, in the dark
          Groped I to find out them, had my desire,
          Fingered their packet, and in fine withdrew
          To mine own room again, making so bold,
          My fears forgetting manners, to unseal
          Their grand commission.   *(V, ii, 4-18)*

Yet the lyrical wealth of the "early" manner has subtle and relevant contributions to make. The musical splendor of the cock ("the trumpet to the morn, . . . with his lofty and shrill-sounding throat") asserts the divine purity of light ("the god of day"). One thinks of Melville's *Cock-a-doodle-doo*, where the clarity and brilliance of the cock's crow symbolizes—though ironically—life's confident color and glory. The cock in *Hamlet* is a quasi-divine messenger, while a complex of opposite implications inheres in the words

Th'extravagant and erring spirit hies
To his confine.

---

11. T. S. Eliot, *"Hamlet,"* in *Selected Essays* (New York: Harcourt, Brace and Company, 1932), pp. 123–24.

Professor L. C. Knights examines these implications—"suggestive tonings," as he calls them. We have, he indicates, reasons to be apprehensive of the Ghost's nature, associated thus with guilt and the infernal world, whereas Hamlet commits himself recklessly to its cause and is undermined by moral evil.[12]

How good or bad King Hamlet had in fact been is a question hardly more tractable than that about the number of Lady Macbeth's children, though he clearly did not die in a state of grace; his admission of torment is part of the shock which so overwhelms his son. In Horatio's speech, "extravagant and erring" is far more sinister than its literal sense of "wandering"; it implies a lawless and willful transgressing of bounds, as, in *Paradise Lost* (VI, 616), Satan's phrase for the good angels recoiling from assault—"somewhat extravagant and wilde"—implies uncontrollable disarray. "Confine" suggests a punishing constriction. To follow the contrast further, the evoking of Christmas holiness (melodiously enriched by the paradox "This bird of dawning singeth all night long") makes absolute—as does the theological dichotomy in *Macbeth*—the opposition between the good things of day and the black agents of night. Horatio's conclusion returns to the early lyrical charm, but again with deeper significance. On this Dover Wilson has commented well: "Russet mantle," he remarks, suggests both dawn's first promise of russet light and the honest countryman in his simple robe, walking over the dew which symbolizes the purity of the natural world as against the nightmarish supernatural.[13] "Wholesome" nights and reviving dawns signalize the goodness of the world's health, of which, as of a lost paradise, so much in the play serves to remind us. A similar early-pastoral touch is felt in

(I, v, 89-90)

The glow-worm shows the matin to be near,
And 'gins to pale his uneffectual fire.

But here the touch probes deeply. The Ghost's tenderness is most moving. "The matin" suggests a religious awakening;

12. L. C. Knights, *An Approach to "Hamlet"* (London: Chatto & Windus, 1960), pp. 45—48.
13. John Dover Wilson, Introduction to *Hamlet* (Cambridge: Cambridge University Press, 1934), p. xxxvi.

"uneffectual fire" is a phrase extraordinary in its pregnancy, yet so economical as to pass almost unnoticed; the insect's quaint and harmless glow contrasts with those "sulph'rous and tormenting flames" to which, his hour being almost come, the spirit must return. In this counterpointing of *A Midsummer Night's Dream* language with tragic horror there is no element of strain. The tenderness is essential to the horror; the play depends on cherished and natural intimacies recalled amid disaster.

How do we take a longer example of this kind of style—the lines in which Gertrude tells how Ophelia died? Some critics find in them a falsetto note which they attribute either to speciousness in Gertrude or to sentimentality in Shakespeare. But let us hear them:

> There is a willow grows askant the brook,
> That shows his hoar leaves in the glassy stream,
> Therewith fantastic garlands did she make
> Of crow-flowers, nettles, daisies, and long purples
> That liberal shepherds give a grosser name,
> But our cold maids do dead men's fingers call them.
> There on the pendent boughs her crownet weeds
> Clamb'ring to hang, an envious sliver broke,
> When down her weedy trophies and herself
> Fell in the weeping brook. Her clothes spread wide,
> And mermaid-like awhile they bore her up,
> Which time she chanted snatches of old lauds,
> As one incapable of her own distress,
> Or like a creature native and indued
> Unto that element. But long it could not be
> Till that her garments, heavy with their drink,
> Pulled the poor wretch from her melodious lay
> To muddy death.
>
> *(IV, vii, 165-82)*

Death by drowning is as highly stylized here as it might be in an operatic aria, with its conceits about the weeping brook and the singing mermaid. But the romance note is relevant, not gratuitous. It links Ophelia with flowers and water, implies her naïve innocence, and sounds a madrigal pathos amidst the darkening tragedy. The aria is artificial, but a valuable effect depends upon it, the evoking (even though in nostalgic idealization) of an innocent world lost in the corruptions of evil, goodness forfeited but lingeringly recalled from oblivion. Realism, a "mature" veracity, would not serve the play's purpose.

A less ambiguous instance occurs in Ophelia's account of her distracted lover:

O, what a noble mind is here o'erthrown!
The courtier's, soldier's, scholar's, eye, tongue, sword,
Th'expectancy and rose of the fair state,
The glass of fashion, and the mould of form,
Th'observed of all observers, quite, quite down,
And I of ladies most deject and wretched,
That sucked the honey of his music vows,
Now see that noble and most sovereign reason
Like sweet bells jangled, out of tune and harsh,
That unmatched form and feature of blown youth,
Blasted with ecstasy! O, woe is me!
(III, i, 153-64) T'have seen what I have seen, see what I see!

This is richly thoughtful like the sonnets, with the courtly and noble music of grief we hear in the mature comedies, but sharpened by tragic power. It vouches for the splendor of the past as against the chaos of the present; contrasting these things, *Hamlet* is like *Othello*.

Some readers hold that Hamlet and Othello—the men, not the plays—both glamourize a deceptive past, which in their naïve confidence they had thought to be good. This is true to the extent that a world which had been taken for good turns out also to encompass evil; it is wisdom's part to know evil but to remain uncorrupted. The good is the supreme value, health the intended condition. So—how do we take the play's evocations of a fine and courtly past? The play is concerned with how we perceive: "there is nothing either good or bad, but thinking makes it so." When Hamlet compares the murdered King with the usurper, and contrasts "Hyperion's curls, the front of Jove himself," with the "mildewed ear," is he falsely idealizing one who, having died unshriven, is being tormented

Till the foul crimes done in my days of nature
(I, v, 12-13) Are burnt and purged away.

Do we agree with Mr. John Vyvyan in *The Shakespearean*

Ethic that Hamlet is a bemused idealizer? "The fact," Mr. Vyvyan remarks, "that Hamlet had already begun to romanticize his father and to hate his uncle reveals to us his most vulnerable point"[14] that is, presumably, that he has distorted his judgment by obsession. This is a possible way to judge how the play contrasts past and present: it is indeed the way Herman Melville took when he modeled his *Pierre* upon *Hamlet* (at a vast remove), and made his young hero pass from absurd sentimentality to suicidal bitterness. Should we deduce, "How wrong Hamlet was about his father! How naïve his idealizations!"? These evoked splendors of the past, some readers have thought, are Hamlet's fantasies, yearnings for the lost bliss of sentimental ignorance. But I interpret the poetry of courtly and romantic retrospect as saying that there really was a good past, and that King Hamlet, the "majesty of buried Denmark," was a good guardian of his land. I do not mean that we should believe this merely because Hamlet says so; the evidence is wider. It is the prevalence of images of disease and corruption now afflicting Denmark so that its state has become that of the "noble substance" poisoned by the "dram of evil." The spirit in which the old order is evoked is not a sentimental gloss but a tribute to a good state; the past was a past of heroism and love, and this is what Ophelia's and Hamlet's speeches say. If the pre-Claudian past is recalled glowingly, the glow is not Hamlet's delusion but Shakespeare's imagining of the good.

Another style which adds its flavor is that of the great histories, strong, practical, and cogent in a way which offsets Hamlet's speculative amplitudes. Here is how act III, scene iii, opens:

King: I like him not, nor stands it safe with us
To let his madness range. Therefore prepare you,
I your commission will forthwith dispatch,
And he to England shall along with you.
The terms of our estate may not endure
Hazard so near's as doth hourly grow
Out of his brows.   *(III,iii,1-7)*

14. John Vyvyan, *The Shakespearean Ethic* (London: Chatto & Windus, 1959), p. 34.

This note is utterly assured. Yet how readily it modulates into another character when Guildenstern obsequiously replies:

> We will ourselves provide.
> Most holy and religious fear it is
> To keep those many many bodies safe
> *(III, iii, 7-10)* That live and feed upon your majesty.

"Most holy and religious fear," "those many many bodies," "that live and feed upon your majesty"; one cannot mistake the tone. When Rosencrantz then expatiates upon kingship:

> The single and peculiar life is bound
> With all the strength and armour of the mind
> *(III, iii, 11-13)* To keep itself from noyance,

and so forth, the cogency heard in Claudius turns into an interesting form of volubility which Granville-Barker defined as "repetition by complement." His comment is noteworthy:

Shakespeare, in *Hamlet*, shows an extraordinary fondness for this device, and employs it, one would say, as carelessly as constantly. It may at times betoken the teeming mind—his own or his character's—finding two words as easily as one, and too eager to be getting on to choose between them. The use of the conjunction makes smooth going for the verse, the familiar form and the bare addition to the meaning easy reading; and even when this last is negligible—as it is, to take four examples out of Hamlet's mouth alone in a single stretch of a single scene, in "book and volume," "grace and mercy," "strange or odd," "love and friending"—the actor's voice can itself colour the second word to a richer implication.[15]

In the addresses by Guildenstern and Rosencrantz Shakespeare, who expresses by similar means Hamlet's abundance of idea, turns the device to the exposure of specious wordiness. A few lines after the King's cogency, this effective subspecies of the play's resourceful fluency occurs. Moreover, Rosencrantz's sycophancy has an effect of Sophoclean irony, for he addresses his discourse on "the cease of majesty" to a fratricidal usurper. The "repetition by complement" works, then, by its very slipperiness of style to signalize the ambiguity of Claudius's position:

15. Granville-Barker, *Prefaces to Shakespeare: Third Series*, p. 205.

> The cess of majesty
> Dies not alone; but like a gulf doth draw
> What's near it with it. O, 'tis a massy wheel
> Fixed on the summit of the highest mount,
> To whose huge spokes ten thousand lesser things
> Are mortised and adjoined, which when it falls,
> Each small annexment, petty consequence,
> Attends the boist'rous ruin. Never alone
> Did the king sigh, but with a general groan.   *(III, iii, 15-23)*

In one light, Rosencrantz and Guildenstern are talking sense about the importance of kingship. Yet after the directness of Claudius, their leisurely amplifications and repetitiousness betray their idiom as that of sycophancy.

Shakespeare is extraordinarily interested in how things are said. There is a singular awareness of speech fashion in *Hamlet*. Hamlet himself parodies the wordy Polonius, the affected Osric, and ranting Laertes, but there are many other subtleties of speech-slanting. The interest goes to the very heart of the ambiguous relationships between the characters. What exactly do the words imply? When Claudius delivers his first speech,

> Though yet of Hamlet our dear brother's death
> The memory be green, and that it us befitted
> To bear our hearts in grief, and our whole kingdom
> To be contracted in one brow of woe,   *(I, ii, 1-4)*

and so on, is his manner that of the effective and courtly monarch (as Professor Wilson Knight has taken it to be),[16] or is it (to quote Granville-Barker) "too well-balanced," "a little too calculated"[17]—even as Professor L. C. Knights remarks, "the tone and accent of Milton's Belial"?[18] The answer is indicated partly by the context (we have just seen the Ghost), and partly by the "repetition by complement" with which he so lavishly glosses the situation:

> Yet so far hath discretion fought with nature,
> That we with wisest sorrow think on him
> Together with remembrance of ourselves:

16. G. Wilson Knight, *The Wheel of Fire* (London: Oxford University Press, 1930), pp. 36–37.

17. Granville-Barker, *Prefaces to Shakespeare: Third Series*, p. 226.

18. Knights, *An Approach to "Hamlet,"* p. 41.

Therefore our sometime sister, now our queen,
Th'imperial jointress to this warlike state,
Have we, as 'twere with a defeated joy,
With an auspicious, and a dropping eye,
With mirth in funeral, and with dirge in marriage,
In equal scale weighing delight and dole,
(I, ii, 5-14) Taken to wife.

The equilibrating virtuosity of this suggests diplomatic hypocrisy of a high order.

    Rhetorical devices which would in earlier plays have been
external are now fully dramatic and integral; Aeneas's tale to
Dido, as Hamlet and the First Player narrate it, has the bold
extravagance of earlier tragedy to frame it as an artifact within
the play's maturity. The mouse-trap play-within-the-play is set
off in naïvely artificial couplets. The line-by-line thrust-and-
parry so showily effective in the histrionic formalism of
Richard III is recalled for a like effect of fencing here:

Queen: Hamlet, thou hast thy father much offended.
Hamlet: Mother, you have my father much offended.
Queen: Come, come, you answer with an idle tongue.
Hamlet: Go, go, you question with a wicked tongue.
Queen: Why, how now, Hamlet?
Hamlet: What's the matter now?
Queen: Have you forgot me?
Hamlet: No, by the rood, not so!
    You are the queen, your husband's brother's wife,
(III, iv, 9-16)   And (would it were not so) you are my mother.

Polonius's precepts to the parting Laertes are satirically qualified by a comparable artifice of form. "The personified *memory* of wisdom no longer actually possessed" (Coleridge's
phrase),[19] they are not unimpressive; as Granville-Barker remarks, "though wiseacre, [Polonius] is no mere babbling fool.
The famous 'precepts' go to a steady measure, to a melody
distinguished enough, if dry."[20] But is not the measure too
steady, the melody too dry, the pattern betrayingly regular?

Give thy thoughts no tongue,
Nor any unproportioned thought his act.

    19. Coleridge, *Shakespearean Criticism*, 1:199.
    20. Granville-Barker, *Prefaces to Shakespeare: Third Series*, p. 223.

Be thou familiar, but by no means vulgar.
Those friends thou hast, and their adoption tried,
Grapple them unto thy soul with hoops of steel,
But do not dull thy palm with entertainment
Of each new-hatched, unfledged courage. Beware
Of entrance to a quarrel, but being in,
Bear't that th' opposéd may beware of thee.
Give every man thy ear, but few thy voice;
Take each man's censure, but reserve thy judgment.
Costly thy habit as thy purse can buy,
But not expressed in fancy; rich, not gaudy.
For the apparel oft proclaims the man.   *(I, iii, 59-72)*

And so they go on—individually telling, collectively facile. In a
play whose characteristic movement is supple and continuous
these measured aphorisms reveal themselves to be inert. The
tabulating linear structure opposes itself to the living flexibility of the play; the inertness is not in the specific contents but
in the repetitive, formal, and sententious manner.

Let us consider the stylistic range another way. *Hamlet*
unites the homeliest realities with the most speculative tendencies of mood and thought; this is its essence. It begins realis-
tically, as all critics have remarked; one accepts the cold, the
dark, the beating bell, the star circling the pole. Coleridge puts
this initial effect admirably:

Compare the easy language of common life in which this
drama opens, with the wild wayward lyric of the opening of
Macbeth. The language is familiar: no poetic descriptions of
night, no elaborate information conveyed. ... It is the language of *sensation* among men who feared no charge of ef-
feminacy for feeling what they felt no want of resolution to
bear. Yet the armour, the dead silence, the watchfulness that
first interrupts it, the welcome relief of guard, the cold, the
broken expressions as of a man's compelled attention to bodi-
ly feelings allowed no man—all excellently accord with and
prepare for the after gradual rise into tragedy.[21]

The fragments of dialogue create a tense expectancy:

Barnardo: Who's there?
Francisco: Nay, answer me. Stand and unfold yourself.

21. Coleridge, *Shakespearean Criticism*, 1:18.

Barnardo: Long live the king!
Francisco: Barnardo?
Barnardo: He.
Francisco: You come most carefully upon your hour.
Barnardo: 'Tis now struck twelve, get thee to bed, Francisco.
Francisco: For this relief much thanks, 'tis bitter cold.
    And I am sick at heart.
Barnardo: Have you had quiet guard?
Francisco: Not a mouse stirring.
Barnardo: Well, good night:
    If you do meet Horatio and Marcellus,
(I, i, 1-13)   The rivals of my watch, bid them make haste.

Shakespeare continues thus, creating the alert, jumpy mood,
and then, having sufficiently aroused us, settles down to what
seems a leisurely retrospect which, on the stroke of the bell, is
broken with tremendous excitement:

Barnardo: Sit down awhile,
    And let us once again assail your ears,
    That are so fortified against our story,
    What we have two nights seen.
Horatio: Well, sit we down,
    And let us hear Barnardo speak of this.
Barnardo: Last night of all,
    When yon same star that's westward from the pole
    Had made his course t'illume that part of heaven
    Where now it burns, Marcellus and myself,
    The bell then beating one—

A ghost appears . . .

(I, i, 30-40) *Marcellus:* Peace, break thee off, look where it comes again!

This tightening, relaxing, and tightening again is masterly, the
very essence of dramatic genius. It is precisely this registration
of the real which, amid all the play's mysteriousness, convinces
us of the ground whereon it stands. Dr. Tillyard cited, to
similar purpose, Marcellus's long query, between the Ghost's
first and second appearances, about the cause of warlike prepa-
rations. This, as Tillyard observes, "forces one to hear the beat
of hammers in the distance as the accompaniment of the
scene, and to bear in our minds the notion of ordinary physical life going on behind the heightened passions of the main

actors."[22]   It   has   often   been   noted   how   concrete
and familiar is much of the content of Hamlet's mind:
"not spacious scenery and nature," Wolfgang Clemen
remarks, "but rather trades and callings, . . . popular games
and technical terms."[23] In respect of Hamlet himself (though,
as we have seen, not of the play's opening), Coleridge thought
differently; for him, Hamlet's thoughts and imaginings are "far
more vivid than his perceptions."[24] The Coleridgean Hamlet
is, as we might have foreseen,

a person, in whose view the external world, and all its incidents and objects, were comparatively dim, and of no interest in themselves, and which began to interest only, when they
were reflected in the mirror of his mind. Hamlet beheld external things in the same way that a man of vivid imagination,
who shuts his eyes, sees what has previously made an impression on his organs.[25]

Yet this overstates the case; by the style's realism and particu-
larity Hamlet the prince and *Hamlet* the play anchor themselves in the world of mankind, perpetually alert to what goes
on, in the court and in the nation.

More than any other of the plays *Hamlet* moves between the
world of body and the world of mind, between physical and
mental states; it belongs, as L. C. Knights observes, to a period
"when Shakespeare was much concerned with the relationship
between the mind, the whole reflective personality, and the
world in which it engages."[26] Emotions are rendered in a
language of vivid specificity; in this respect reading the play is
virtually equivalent to seeing it. Ophelia describes Hamlet's
distraction as follows:

My lord, as I was sewing in my closet,
Lord Hamlet with his doublet all unbraced,
No hat upon his head, his stockings fouled,
Ungart'red, and down-gyved to his ankle,
Pale as his shirt, his knees knocking each other,
And with a look so piteous in purport

22. Tillyard, *Shakespeare's Problem Plays*, p. 29.
23. Clemen, *The Development of Shakespeare's Imagery*, p. 108.
24. Coleridge, *Shakespearean Criticism*, 1:34.
25. Ibid., 2:150.
26. Knights, *An Approach to "Hamlet,"* p. 12.

As if he had been looséd out of hell
(II, i, 74-81) To speak of horrors—he comes before me.

When Hamlet sees the Ghost in his mother's room, Gertrude
describes his dread with dramatic vividness:

Forth at your eyes your spirits wildly peep,
And as the sleeping soldiers in th'alarm,
(III, iv, 119- Your bedded hairs like life in excrements
22) Start up and stand an end.

Physical and mental states have a peculiarly searching interrela-
tionship in a play where because of mental distress the majestical roof fretted with golden fire turns to a foul and pestilent
congregation of vapours, and man, the paragon of animals,
becomes the quintessence of dust; a play where Hamlet could
be bounded in a nutshell and count himself king of infinite
space were it not that he has bad dreams. Emotional, mental,
or intellectual operations always take on a physical language in
Shakespeare, but here, where by the nature of the hero so
much is conceptualized, recurrence to the concrete is peculiarly significant. So "the native hue of resolution / Is sicklied o'er
with the pale cast of thought," and we perceive the health of
the determined countenance yield before the pallor of reflection. For Hamlet thought has become, through the discovery of
evil, a baffling and weakening of purpose, not a clarifying and
strengthening of it. "Leave her to heaven," the Ghost instructs
Hamlet, of Gertrude's remorse,

And to those thorns that in her bosom lodge
(I, v, 86-88) To prick and sting her.

And we feel, intensely concentrated, the pangs the mind in-
flicts on the body, the physical anguish of conscience.

The play, then, grounds itself perpetually on the practical,
the immediate, the realistic; thence it makes its reconnaissance
into the intense, the distracted, the speculative, indeed the
extravagant. Hyperbole is a frequent Shakespearean device, allowing a fine fling, a lavish contrast to the practical-moderate.
The Ghost's disclosure of what he may not disclose is so vivid,
so hyperbolic, as almost to parody the horrific:

But that I am forbid
To tell the secrets of my prison-house,

I could a tale unfold whose lightest word
Would harrow up thy soul, freeze thy young blood,
Make thy two eyes likes stars start from their spheres,
Thy knotted and combinéd locks to part,
And each particular hair to stand an end,
Like quills upon the fretful porpentine.   *(I, v, 13-20)*

But, he goes on,

        this eternal blazon may not be
To ears of flesh and blood.   *(I, v, 21-22)*

a reticence which qualifies his speech as the most sensational noncommunication in literature. My point is that this hyperbolic lavishness remains sharp and telling, imaginatively focused and realized. Whatever amplitudes the writing offers, it remains intent, superbly specific. The terms in which King Hamlet describes his death are both hyperbolic and precise:

        Sleeping within my orchard,
My custom always of the afternoon,
Upon my secure hour thy uncle stole
With juice of cursed hebona in a vial,
And in the porches of my ears did pour
The leperous distilment, whose effect
Holds such an enmity with blood of man
That swift as quicksilver it courses through
The natural gates and alleys of the body,
And with a sudden vigour it doth posset
And curd, like eager droppings into milk,
The thin and wholesome blood; so did it mine,
And a most instant tetter barked about
Most lazar-like with vile and loathsome crust
All my smooth body.   *(I, v, 59-73)*

The syntax is fluent and lithe, phrase generating phrase with an easy and supple velocity, the movement evolving rapidly like the purposeful stealth and "sudden vigour" of the action, the rhythms actualizing the deed. The remarkable mimetic power of this style seems to be displayed effortlessly; the expressive details—"porches of my ears," "swift as quicksilver," "natural gates and alleys," "posset/And curd," "eager droppings into milk"—flow swiftly along on a current of informative idea, and finally bring out the physical sensation so sharply, in the consonantal attack of

a most instant tetter barked about
Most lazar-like with vile and loathsome crust
All my smooth body,

that one feels the erupting sores in one's own flesh, so vividly contrasted with the almost sensual tenderness of "All my smooth body."

Rich, precise, and full as it is, the poetry has a remarkable plasticity, a mercurial responsiveness. It must follow swift evolutions of idea, and this it does. It was this quality Hazlitt was getting at when he criticized Kemble and Kean for acting Hamlet too stiffly:

The character of Hamlet is made up of undulating lines; it has the yielding flexibility of "a wave o'th' sea." Mr. Kemble plays it like a man in armour, with a determined inveteracy of purpose, in one undeviating straight line, which is as remote from the natural grace and refined susceptibility of the character, as the sharp angles and abrupt starts which Mr. Kean introduces into the part.[27]

Hamlet's natural grace and susceptibility promote his undulating volubility; he himself recognizes this as an indulgence, and until late in the play the intoxication of expression serves him in place of wisdom—but in this lies his fascination for us. Yet fluidity and amplitude, "repetition by complement," are not Hamlet's alone; Shakespeare seems to have felt everywhere that language should run like quicksilver through the natural gates and alleys of meaning, exploring all parts of an idea by mercurial semantics.

Fluidity is the language of exploratory and flexible intelligence; the world of the play is not one of fixities and definites but one in which a watchful and speculative tentativeness is the proper response. Even the steady Horatio shares this quality. How extraordinarily supple and mimetic is the syntax of his first long speech:

27. William Hazlitt, "Characters of Shakespeare's Plays," in *The Complete Works of William Hazlitt*, ed. P. P. Howe (London and Toronto: J. M. Dent, 1930–34), 4:237.

> Our last king,
> Whose image even but now appeared to us,
> Was as you know by Fortinbras of Norway,
> Thereto pricked on by a most emulate pride,
> Dared to the combat; in which our valiant Hamlet
> (For so this side of our known world esteemed him)
> Did slay this Fortinbras, who by a sealed compact,
> Well ratified by law and heraldry,
> Did forfeit (with his life) all those his lands
> Which he stood seized of, to the conqueror,
> Against the which a moiety competent
> Was gagéd by our king, which had returned
> To the inheritance of Fortinbras,
> Had he been vanquisher; as by the same co-mart,
> And carriage of the article designed,
> His fell to Hamlet.   *(I, i, 80-95)*

Shakespeare's earlier plays, to be sure, had not lacked eloquent speakers—Berowne on the "true Promethean fire" of love, Faulconbridge on "Commodity," Portia on mercy, Hotspur on the popinjay lord, Jaques on the world as a stage, and so on. But in all these there is a vigorous onward drive of idea; they know what they want to say. In *Hamlet* there is, rather, a fascinated desire in all characters to know what it is they are defining. How lithe, voluble, mimetically responsive to the reciprocations of the treaty Horatio's explanation is; how probingly diplomatic, steering through mixed motives and expediencies, is Claudius's opening speech; how fertile in reflection is even the forthright Laertes as he warns Ophelia against Hamlet, expanding into general morals, contracting to the particular case, throwing aphorisms in, circling repeatedly over his meanings, until Ophelia is provoked to a demure but pithy rejoinder! *Hamlet* is a play of exhilarating words in which the speakers are engaged in an endless search after comprehension; they try incessantly to cast the exact line of definition round their utterances, and in doing this they look at their notions in multiple lights:

> the main motive of our preparations,
> The source of this our watch, and the chief head
> Of this post-haste and romage in the land . . .   *(I, i, 105-7)*

the like precurse of fierce events,
As harbingers preceding still the fates,
(I, i, 117-19) And prologue to the omen coming on.

Of life, of crown, of queen at once dispatched,
Cut off even in the blossoms of my sin,
Unhouseled, disappointed, unaneled,
No reck'ning made, but sent to my account
(I, v, 75-79) With all my imperfections on my head.

The spirit of this is Schücking's "baroque exuberance"; yet the
effect is less the baroque intention of exuberance for exuberance's sake than the desire, in a bewildering world, that
through words the mind's phantasmagoria should be defined
and grasped. This, in a way, is Gertrude Stein's famous quip—
"How do I know what I think till I see what I say?" This is
done not by overt debate, but by juxtaposing complex
thoughts and feelings. To quote Mr. Derek Traversi,

Hamlet's soliloquies are far less "rationalized" than Ulysses'
discussions. The laborious machinery of ratiocination is replaced by subtle and truly dramatic shifts of feeling. In the
"To be or not to be" speech ... Hamlet's contrasted moods
are *felt in the movement of the verse,* in language that reflects
through the varied and precise operation of the senses the
constantly fluctuating relation of thought to emotion. More
ample resources of language are being brought into play. We
feel the sharp immediacy of the vernacular ("To *grunt* and
sweat under a weary life") contrasted with the remote Latinity
of "quietus" and "consummation." The conflicts in Hamlet's
mind are no longer arguments but *states* of experience in
which sense and thought are fused in the study not of an idea
but of a character.[28]

The parallel would be not with the intellectual formulations of
Troilus and Cressida but with Macbeth's meditations on murder, where we are at the very edge of language as it distin-
guishes possibilities under the impulsive pressure of emotion.

To conclude: That the poetic style of *Hamlet* is brilliant
and imaginative needs no demonstrating. Here Shakespeare's
style reaches the fullest possible realization of its meaning

28. Derek A. Traversi, *An Approach to Shakespeare*, 2d ed.
(Garden City, N. Y.: Doubleday, 1957), pp. 82–83.

while still remaining fertile and unstrained. Professor Clemen
has noted this of the imagery:

Hamlet's way of employing images is unique in Shakespeare's
drama. When he begins to speak, the images fairly stream to
him without the slightest effort—not as similes or conscious
paraphrases, but as immediate and spontaneous visions.[29]

As with his creation, so with the creator: to Shakespeare's
mind too there stream (the word fits the swiftness and wealth
of effect) the materials of the play, those dual worlds of practical reality and conceptual probing, those psychic contrasts of
health and illness, wholeness and corruption, past and present,
outward show and inward query, deceptive knowledge and
bewildered discovery, which are the play's particular effects.
Let me end with one whole speech, that in which Hamlet
addresses his father's spirit. Try transferring it to Brutus before
the ghost of Caesar, or Macbeth before the ghost of Banquo,
and you will feel how much the special language of *Hamlet* is
this melodious, grandiloquent, impulsive, fluent, rapidly evolving style, circling swiftly round its ideas, voluble yet exact,
majestically masterly, yet in its shifts of rhythm intently alert
to the thoughts and feelings it so intimately discloses. This, as
nearly as any passage, gives the essentials of *Hamlet's* styles:

Angels and ministers of grace defend us!
Be thou a spirit of health, or goblin damned,
Bring with thee airs from heaven, or blasts from hell,
Be thy intents wicked, or charitable,
Thou com'st in such a questionable shape
That I will speak to thee. I'll call thee Hamlet,
King, father, royal Dane. O, answer me!
Let me not burst in ignorance, but tell
Why thy canonized bones hearséd in death
Have burst their cerements? why the sepulchre,
Wherein we saw thee quietly inurned,
Hath oped his ponderous and marble jaws
To cast thee up again? What may this mean
That thou, dead corse, again in complete steel
Revisits thus the glimpses of the moon,
Making night hideous, and we fools of nature

29. Clemen, *The Development of Shakespeare's Imagery*, p. 106.

So horridly to shake our disposition
(I, iv, 39 56)   With thoughts beyond the reaches of our souls?

No wonder that, for most people, *Hamlet* is the play of plays. These speeches, as Hazlitt says, "are as real as our own thoughts. Their reality is in the reader's mind."[30]

---

30. Hazlitt, "Characters of Shakespeare's Plays," 4:232.

Command, Question, and Assertion in *King Lear*

MADELEINE DORAN

3

When King Lear walks on the stage within a few lines of the
opening of the play, he addresses the court with a declaration
of his intentions, much of it cast in the imperative mood:

Meantime we shall express our darker purpose.
Give me the map there. Know we have divided
In three our kingdom; and 'tis our fast intent
To shake all cares and business from our age,
Conferring them on younger strengths while we
Unburthen'd crawl toward death.[1]   *(I, i, 38-42)*

He has struck at once his own most characteristic syntactical
mood, and with it one of the distinguishing moods of the
tragedy, for it is Lear's voice which will dominate the play. In
no other Shakespearean tragedy do we hear so imperious a
voice—so continually demanding, ordering, exclaiming, im-
precating, pronouncing.

When one looks closely at the syntax of the play, one discovers some interesting things. One observes that several types
of sentences recur, and that these make a pattern quite unlike
that in any other of the tragedies. *Othello*, another play which
I have analyzed in detail, has a similarly recurrent but very
different syntactical pattern.[2] It is exciting to discover how
sensitive a means syntax may be—as we already know diction,
imagery, and meter to be—in creating the distinctive tone of a

---

1. Shakespeare quotations are from the Kittredge edition (Boston,
1940).
2. "Iago's 'if': An Essay on the Syntax of *Othello*," in *The Drama
of the Renaissance: Essays for Leicester Bradner*, ed. Elmer M. Blistein
(Providence, R. I.: Brown University Press, 1970), pp. 69-99.

play. No one of Shakespeare's great tragedies sounds quite like any other.

Lear's most characteristic note is the note of command, whether the syntax be formally in the imperative mood ("Know this!" "Do that!") or whether it be in some other. A variant of the imperative is the "Let it be done" or "May it be done" construction, which takes the place of the Latin hortative or imperative subjunctive. Lear uses this construction frequently as a form of command ("Let me not stay a jot for dinner!" [I, iv, 8]) or of urgent wish, as in his prayers to the gods: "O, let me not be mad, not mad, sweet heaven! Keep me in temper" (I, v, 49-50). Even the indicative mood is for him often a declaration of unalterable intention, expressive of the same dominance of will as in the commands:

> The barbarous Scythian
> . . . shall to my bosom
> Be as well neighbour'd, pitied, and reliev'd,
> As thou my sometime daughter.

(I, i, 118-22)

If we listen sensitively, we shall also become aware in Lear's part of two other common types of sentence, both in the indicative mood. One is the interrogative sentence, variously used; the other the declarative sentence used for simple, unqualified assertions.

Let us return to the first scene, in which the pattern of syntax is set. Lear follows his announcement of retiring from government and of dividing his kingdom among his three daughters with a planned ceremony. He asks each of the daughters in turn how much she loves him. These questions are not truly queries, but demands; they are asked to dramatize the gift-giving, not to learn the answers, which he thinks he knows already.

> Tell me, my daughters
> . . . .
> Which of you shall we say doth love us most?
> That we our largest bounty may extend
> Where nature doth with merit challenge? Goneril,
> Our eldest-born, speak first.

(I, i, 49-55)

Goneril makes a fulsome reply, that she loves him better than eyesight, space, and liberty, no less than life, grace, health, beauty, honor; and Lear marks off her portion on the map. He next puts the question to Regan:

> What says our second daughter,
> Our dearest Regan, wife to Cornwall? Speak   *(I, i, 68-69)*

receives a similar fulsome reply (that she takes no joy in anything but her father's love), and in turn designates her portion. Then he questions Cordelia:

> Now, our joy,
> Although the last, not least; . . .
> . . . what can you say to draw
> A third more opulent than your sisters? Speak.   *(I, i, 84-88)*

Clearly he had intended the best portion for her. Note the dialogue which follows the question to her.

> Nothing, my lord.
> Nothing?
> Nothing.
> Nothing can come of nothing. Speak again!   *(I, i, 89-92)*

Lear's question, "Nothing? " is one of shocked incredulity. The declaration, "Nothing can come of nothing," is a flat assertion of an apparent truism: Nihil ex nihilo. The use of the interrogative in Lear's part is to vary from such demanding or exclamatory questions early in the play to questions of genuine inquiry later on. The declarative sentence will continue to be used for plain unqualified assertions, often aphoristic or sententious, but later these will be reflections of new experience, not just automatic responses to a situation.

Back to the dialogue between Lear and Cordelia. To his angry order, "Speak again." she replies in a statement which seems clear and is yet a riddle—a profound one, the answer to which is not to be learned until nearly the end of the play:

> Unhappy that I am, I cannot heave
> My heart into my mouth. I love your majesty
> According to my bond; no more nor less.   *(I, i, 93-95)*

His question put in terms of quantity has begot a reply in kind, and Goneril's and Regan's insincere protestations of love have provoked a sarcastic nicety of distinction in Cordelia's terms:

> Why have my sisters husbands, if they say
> They love you all? ...
> Sure I shall never marry like my sisters,
> To love my father all.

(I, i, 101-6)

Her statement is followed by another balanced interchange of question and answer:

> *Lear:* But goes thy heart with this?
> *Cor:*   Ay, my good lord.
> *Lear:* So young, and so untender?
> *Cor:* So young, my lord, and true.

(I, i, 107-9)

The awful fiat of disinheritance, attested by a frightening oath, follows at once:

> Let it be so! thy truth then be thy dower!
> For, by the sacred radiance of the sun,
> The mysteries of Hecate and the night;
> By all the operation of the orbs
> From whom we do exist and cease to be;
> Here I disclaim all my paternal care,
> Propinquity and property of blood,
> And as a stranger to my heart and me
> Hold thee from this for ever.

(I, i, 110-18)

The syntactical patterns of command, question, and assertion have been established. The three themes—to use a strictly musical metaphor—have been stated. As the play progresses, they will be varied and developed in complex harmonies and dissonances until they are brought to a resolution at the end.

We might say that these matters of syntax are just a matter of character. But we have heard Cordelia's plain assertions balancing Lear's plain questions ("Nothing?" "Nothing"; "So young and so untender?" "So young, my lord, and true"). Moreover, Lear's voice is not the only one in which we are to hear commands, hortatory prayers, emphatic assertions of intent, astonished questions, and sententious declarations. Listen to Kent, for instance, expostulating with Lear on his fatal decision to divide his kingdom and banish Cordelia:

> Be Kent unmannerly
> When Lear is mad. What wouldst thou do, old man?
> Think'st thou that duty shall have dread to speak

When power to flattery bows? To plainness honour's bound
When majesty falls to folly. Reverse thy doom;
And in thy best consideration check
This hideous rashness.   *(I, i, 147-53)*

And again,

> Revoke thy gift,
> Or, whilst I can vent clamour from my throat,
> I'll tell thee thou dost evil.   *(I, i, 167-69)*

It is extraordinary to what a degree the syntax of other
speakers in the play reflects Lear's. Goneril and Regan are
busy with commands; so are Gloucester and, later, Edmund.
Cordelia's prayers—if different in tone from her father's, having more in them of supplication than of command—are yet
like his in syntax:

> All blest secrets,
> All you unpublish'd virtues of the earth,
> Spring with my tears! be aident and remediate
> In the good man's distress!   *(IV, iv, 15-18)*

So likewise are Gloucester's prayers: "Kind gods, forgive me
that and prosper him!" (III, vii, 92). And Gloucester's questions are as amazed as Lear's.[3] Edgar's and Cordelia's are as
full of shock at the discovery of unwelcome truths.[4] Goneril,
Regan, and Cornwall ask questions, too—not in wonder, however, but in hatred; they turn questions into torturing inter-
rogations.[5] The Fool is always asking questions for the sake of
the gnomic or parabolic answers he supplies to them.[6] Unqualified assertions on everybody's part are the commonest
type of declarative sentence in the play. Kent, Edgar, and
Albany can be at times as aphoristic as Lear.[7]

---

3. "Kent banish'd thus? and France in choler parted?" (I, ii,
23-26); and note the rest of the dialogue between Gloucester and Edmund in this scene. For another hortatory prayer, see IV, i, 67-72.
4. For example, Edgar's "O gods! Who is't can say 'I am at the
worst'? / I am worse than e'er I was" (IV, i, 25-26), and Cordelia's "Was
this a face/To be oppos'd against the warring winds?" introducing a
series of shocked questions on her sisters' treatment of Lear (IV, vii,
31-40).
5. Illustrated below, pp. 66-67, 72-73.
6. See below, pp. 64-65.
7. For example, Edgar in his two reflective soliloquies (III, vi, 108

The fact that these types of sentences are repeated to some degree in the speech of other characters than Lear indicates that they are not limited in function to the distinguishing of character. Lear's syntax does indeed reflect his. It is the primary means by which we are made aware of his temperament and habits of mind; or, put more critically, it is the primary means by which a dramatic character called Lear is created. But in what it suggests the syntax goes beyond anything Shakespeare wants to have us understand about Lear himself. It is an important means by which we enter (on a deeper level than formulated ideas) the peculiar universe of this play; for the universe of the play is artistic as well as moral. Possibly this is a way of saying that the universe of the play is the same as Lear's universe. But in any case what is suggested is something beyond "character" in the ordinary, limited sense of the term. The "world" of a tragedy is created not only by what is said but by how it is said. Scrutiny will show that the grammatical structure has as much to do as the other resources of the language—diction, imagery, figure, prosody—in creating the universe of this tragedy. And I think this is because the syntax is so intimately appropriate to the fable, as Shakespeare conceived it.

The Lear story is a folktale at base. The essence of the tale is that in a test of love of his three daughters, a father fails to understand the riddling answer of the youngest: "I love you as much as salt"; he must learn the value of salt by being deprived of it before he realizes that this youngest daughter is the only one who loves him truly. Although the old story was moved into a political context by Geoffrey of Monmouth's graft of it in the twelfth century on British legendary history, and although it was further sophisticated in its subsequent retellings in the chronicle and in drama, the folktale motifs of the love test, the youngest-best, and a riddle answerable only

ff.; IV, i, 1 ff.) and in his response to the sight of his blinded father (IV, i, 27-28); Albany in dialogue with Goneril (IV, ii, 29 ff.); Kent in response to Lear (I, i, 150-51, 155-56); in reflections on his and Lear's state (II, ii, 167-69, 172-73); and on the stars (IV, iv, 34-35). For emphatic assertion, not sententious, note Kent's unflattering portrait of Oswald (II,ii, 15 ff.) and of Oswald's kind (II, ii, 78 ff.).

after experience, remained a part of it.[8] And so did they in Shakespeare. He did nothing to obliterate the motifs and conventions of folk or fairy tale; in fact, they determined his artistic point of view in the handling of action, character, and even language. The story from Sidney's *Arcadia* which he used to parallel and complicate the Lear plot, the story of the old king of Paphlagonia and his two sons,[9] whom Shakespeare turned into Gloucester, Edgar, and Edmund, helped him to expand the universal meaning of the Lear story and convert it to tragedy. In the *Arcadia* the episode of the Paphlagonian king was a moral exemplum on the theme of kindness and unkindness, that is, of naturalness and unnaturalness in filial relations. Shakespeare enlarged the theme to encompass the breaking of bonds on all levels of relationship: between father and child, brother and brother, sister and sister, king and subject, man and the gods. He changed Cordelia's riddle, the old loving-like-salt riddle, which in Geoffrey had become, "As much as thou hast, so much thou art worth, and so much I love thee,"[10] to

8. For the full history of the story consult Wilfrid Perrett, *The Story of King Lear from Geoffrey of Monmouth to Shakespeare* (Berlin, 1904) (*Palaestra* XXXV); for a summary of the case for the versions Shakespeare appears to have known, including Geoffrey, see pp. 272-89.

9. *Arcadia*, 1590, in *Works*, ed. Albert Feuillerat (Cambridge: Cambridge University Press, 1922), 2:10.

10. "Etenim quantum habes, tantum vales, tantumque te diligo." As Perrett long ago pointed out (*The Story of King Lear*, pp. 14-15, 228-40), only Geoffrey, the first teller of the story as we know it, motivated Cordelia's double-edged riddling reply to her father in her acuteness and wit as well as in her honesty. Aware that her father has been taken in by the exaggerated protestations of her sisters, Geoffrey's "Cordeilla" wishes to try him herself ("tentare illum cupiens"), and she frames an answer which both glances at their speeches and is a test of his understanding. She cannot believe that any daughter would dare to admit she loved her father more than a father, unless she were striving to conceal the truth in jesting words ("nisi jocosis verbis veritatem celare nitatur"). As for herself she has always loved him as a father and always will. Although he persists in wringing more from her ("a me magis extorquere"), let him hear the truth of her love and put an end to his questions: "In truth, as much as thou hast, so much art thou worth, and so much I love thee." Lear, believing she spoke from the fullness of her heart, became vehemently angry and disinherited her forthwith. (Passage quoted in full in Perrett, p. 14, n. 1 and p. 228.) Omissions (especially of the "nisi . . . nitatur" and "pater ratus eam ex abundantia cordis dixisse" phrases) and changes of emphasis in the later versions of the tale, including Holinshed's, show that the tellers all missed the point

"I love you according to my bond." And he deepened the theme to sound the very nature of love.

It will be seen that the generally not very complicated syntax of the play—with its plain and emphatic declaratives, its commanding or hortatory imperatives—fits the fairy-tale world of absolutes: good and evil, truth and falsehood, love and hate. In a fairy tale, also, questions are posed for the sake of answers, which are either gnomic or riddling; the riddles must contain some element of ambiguity or irony and must not be understood until the hero has discovered their meaning by a test or by experience. In the Henry plays, and in tragedies conceived in more realistic terms, such as *Julius Caesar* and *Coriolanus*, there is a good deal of persuasive argument, logical or emotional, before decisions are made or altered. Deliberative rhetoric requires a complex and varied syntax for the consideration of possibilities, the weighing of alternatives, the nice adjustment of principle to expediency. But in *King Lear*, the King has made his first decision, to divide his kingdom and give up the responsibility of governing it, before the play opens; he makes his second one, to banish Cordelia and divide her portion between the other two daughters and sons-in-law, without deliberation. The action in the main plot, after he has made the second, and fatal, decision, is a series of shocking and explosive confrontations, not of events arising from earlier decisions and leading to new ones. Lear has, indeed, surrendered the possibility of further free decision. His part, until late in the play, is therefore passive in the strict sense of the word; he can do nothing but suffer in the process of learning and accepting his mistake.

The intrigues of the sisters and of Edmund which carry the action forward are quickly motivated, simply conceived, and easily managed. The intrigue of Edmund against his brother is even crude, without much attention to plausibility in detail. Much of the preparation for the denouement, such as the part played by Kent and Gloucester in the return of Cordelia to aid her father, is merely hinted at, never worked out. For this kind of plot, where motivation is often taken for granted, creduli-

as much as Geoffrey's Lear; the "quantum habes" riddle became shocking if not unintelligible. Although Shakespeare altered the riddle significantly, his Cordelia is closest to Geoffrey's in acuteness and spirit.

ty is stressed, emotion is unshaded, action is unsubtle, and persuasion is by force, no very complex or subtle syntax is wanted. This is not to say that the play is smooth in the hearing or reading. Far from it. Boldness in diction, grammar, trope, and meter make the going slow and sometimes rough. Much of the style is craggy. But it is not often complex sentences that make it so.[11]

It is interesting to note that conditional sentences, which in *Othello* accompany every significant move in the action, are relatively sparse in *King Lear*. The very core of Othello's tragedy is his betrayal by false conditions, which he is made to believe are true; the conditional sentences in his part and in Iago's occur in nearly every possible grammatical variation in the indicative and subjunctive moods. In *King Lear* conditional sentences occur largely in the parts of the Fool and of the plotting characters, i.e., Edmund, Goneril, and Regan. Their special purpose in the Fool's part I shall return to a little later. In the "practisers'" parts they remind us merely of the possibilities recognized and exploited by the opportunist: "If he distaste it, let him to our sister" (I, iii, 14), or "If I find him comforting the King, it will stuff his suspicion more fully" (III, v, 21-22). These are very like the similar ones Iago speaks in soliloquy as he improvises his successive moves against Othello. It is significant, surely, that there are few conditional sentences in the speeches of Lear, and that those few are memorable.[12] The world the King inhabits at the beginning of the play is a world of certainties and absolutes, not a world of uncertainties or contingencies. Within the reach of his power

11. An exception which proves the rule is Goneril's veiled threat to her father that he had better reduce his train or face the consequences: "Sir, I had thought, by making this well known to you," etc. (I, iv, 223 ff.); it is a masterpiece of syntactical indirection in the conditional subjunctive.

12. Note especially the two in his first curse on Goneril (I, iv, 297-311), the "Hear, Nature, hear!" speech. Since the intent of the curse is to make Goneril sterile, he prays Nature not to fulfill the normal possibility that she have a child: "Suspend thy purpose, if thou didst intend/ To make this creature fruitful." The restatement of the condition to cover this possibility, "If she must teem,/ Create her child of spleen, . . ." is as much an extension of the horror of his curse as it is a recognition of a deity with intentions he cannot be certain of; it is a second thought inviting a more precise and fitting retribution on his own ungrateful child.

his commands bring obedience. To him it is a clearly defined world of privileges and obligations, without conditions or doubts. He never says: "If this were so, I should do such and such," but always, "Let this be so."

Lear's discovery through experience is in part a discovery of the world of contingency, in which conditions govern all relations. Perhaps he did not so much fail to recognize contingency as to suppose that he alone could set all the conditions. The most crucial condition he discovers is that his authority and the respect he assumes to be due him under the title of king— "the name, and all th' additions to a king"—are not absolute, but are contingent on his power. That given away, his commands are worthless. When "the sway, revenue, execution of the rest" are gone, his "additions" disappear. He is later to extend his discovery to other experiences than his own—for instance, to the general realm of justice:

> Plate sin with gold,
> And the strong lance of justice hurtless breaks;
> Arm it in rags, a pygmy's straw does pierce it.

(IV, vi, 169-71)

But Lear does at the start believe in at least one contingency, that love is given in proportion to benefits received. This means that he has things precisely upside down. What Cordelia's love will teach him is that love is the one true absolute, given without measure and without condition.

The conflict in Lear's mind, therefore, is not a debate leading to decision, but a resistance to discovery of unwelcome truths. The syntactical form which counterpoints his imperatives is the question in the indicative mood. The counterpointing begins with his shocked question to Cordelia, when the first crack appears in the certainties of his world. "Nothing, my lord." "Nothing?" As other cracks appear and deepen, the incredulous exclamatory questions ("Are you our daughter?") shade into questions about his own identity as father and as king ("Who is it that can tell me who I am?"). These give place, as his experience teaches him more, to general questions on human society and the nature of man. To some of his questions he supplies the answers with the aphoristic assertions I have mentioned. They are not necessarily the right answers.

These must be found, if at all, in the implications of the tragedy as a whole.

   To follow the varied use of these sentence patterns throughout the play we should need to have the text in front of us and
ample time to study it in. We have neither. The lecture is brief,
and you have only your ears to follow me with. All I can hope
to do is to throw into relief, in the principal scenes of the Lear
plot, the interplay and function of the three "themes" (to
revert to the musical metaphor) and so to indicate the direction the development takes.

   Lear makes the first discovery of his mistake in his stipu-
lated monthly sojourn at Goneril's castle (I, iii, iv). You will
recall that she orders her servants to "come slack of" their
services to him, picks a quarrel with him over his hundred
attendant knights, threatens that if he does not reduce their
number she will do it herself, makes it appear that the knights
are quarreling and brawling, but actually sees to it that her
servants stir up trouble so that she may "breed from hence
occasions" to complain. This behavior is so incredible to Lear,
considering that he has given her half his kingdom, that he
demands of her who she is ("Are you our daughter?" and
"Your name, fair gentlewoman?" [I, iv, 238, 257]) and who
he is:

Doth any here know me? This is not Lear.
Doth Lear walk thus? speak thus? Where are his eyes?
Either his notion weakens, his discernings
Are lethargied—Ha! waking? 'Tis not so!
Who is it that can tell me who I am?   *(I, iv, 246-50)*

The Fool knows the answer, and interposes sotto voce, "Lear's
shadow." Lear's questions are put sarcastically, in exasperated
frustration, but beneath them is the deeper note of uncertain
identity. If he is not recognized as father and as king, then
who is he? Who is Lear if he is not these things? He calls for
his horses to be saddled that he may ride off to Regan's, and in
the most terrible curse in the play calls down on Goneril the
retributive judgment of Nature, that she be sterile; or, if not,
that her child

     be a thwart disnatur'd torment to her.
Let it stamp wrinkles in her brow of youth,

With cadent tears fret channels in her cheeks,
Turn all her mother's pains and benefits
To laughter and contempt, that she may feel
How sharper than a serpent's tooth it is
(I, iv, 305-11) To have a thankless child!

His discovery that Goneril had already dismissed half his train
of knights before she even requested him to do it brings down
on her another curse. Then Lear storms out with the emphatic
assertion, "Yet have I left a daughter" (l. 327), and a threat of
vengeance.

But something else has been going on in this scene. The
Fool has been asking Lear questions, in the form of posers
or riddles so that he may supply the witty answers. Since
they are all variations on the theme of Lear's folly in giving up
his crown or of banishing the wrong daughter, they emphasize
the same truths that Lear's own questions of vexed astonish-
ment show him so reluctant to accept.

Fool: . . . Can you make no use of nothing, nuncle?
(I, iv, 143-46) *Lear:* Why, no, boy, Nothing can be made out of nothing.

We have heard this before. The Fool gives the axiom a new
twist:

Prithee tell him, so much the rent of his land comes to.
(I, iv, 147-49) He will not believe a fool.

Lear's comment, "A bitter fool," prompts a new question:

Fool: Dost thou know the difference, my boy, between a
    bitter fool and a sweet fool?
Lear: No, lad, teach me.
Fool: That lord that counsell'd thee
        To give away thy land,
    Come place him here by me
        Do thou for him stand.
    The sweet and bitter fool
        Will presently appear;
    The one in motley here,
        The other found out there.
Lear: Dost thou call me fool, boy?
Fool: All thy other titles thou hast
(I, iv, 151-64)   given away; that thou wast born with.

Sometimes the situation is reversed and Lear asks the question, as at the end of the preceding passage, but the interchange is only a variant on the same riddling game.

Fool: ... How now, nuncle? Would I had two coxcombs and two daughters!
Lear: Why, my boy?
Fool: If I gave them all my living, I'ld keep my coxcombs *(I, iv, 117-* myself. There's mine! beg another of thy daughters. *22)*

The Fool's answers, like the last one, are full of "if's," for it is precisely the world of contingency that he is teaching Lear about. "Nay," he says to Kent, "an thou canst not smile as the wind sits, thou'lt catch cold shortly. ... if thou follow him thou must needs wear my coxcomb" (ll. 112-17). The Fool's parabolic riddles[13] and plain assertions of obvious truths are choric in effect; but they also perhaps suggest what is running in Lear's own mind, for at one point he recognizes his dreadful mistake:

         O most small fault,
How ugly didst thou in Cordelia show!
Which, like an engine, wrench'd my frame of nature
From the fix'd place; drew from my heart all love
And added to the gall. O Lear, Lear, Lear!
Beat at this gate that let thy folly in
And thy dear judgment out! *(I, iv, 288-94)*

    Warned by Goneril of Lear's departure, Regan and her husband leave home to afford an excuse for not taking her father in; and it is at Gloucester's castle that father, daughter, and son-in-law meet. In this scene (II, iv) we hear again the incredulous questions,

Deny to speak with me? They are sick? they are weary?
They have travell'd all the night? Mere fetches— *(II, iv, 89-90)*

the angry imprecations,

You nimble lightnings, dart your blinding flames
Into her scornful eyes! Infect her beauty,

----

13. For example, in addition to those quoted, "Give me an egg, nuncle, and I'll give thee two crowns" (I, iv, 170 ff.), "Canst tell how an oyster makes his shell? " (I, v, 26-34), and so on.

(II, iv, 167-
70)

> You fen-suck'd fogs, drawn by the pow'rful sun,
> To fall and blast her pride!

But there is now a marked difference from the earlier scenes, for Lear slips from the offensive to the defensive. He now tries, with evidence of increasing inner stress, to maintain a front against a truth too dreadful for him to acknowledge: that his second daughter, as the Fool had predicted, tastes as like the first "as a crab does to a crab." He keeps insisting, against all the signs—the sight of Kent his messenger in the stocks, Cornwall's and Regan's refusal at first to see him, Regan's coldness when she does—that his daughter's eyes "Do comfort, and not burn," that it is not in her to cut off his train or "oppose the bolt" against his coming in, that she better knows "the offices of nature, bond of childhood,/Effects of courtesy, dues of gratitude" (ll. 173-84). Throughout the scene he struggles to keep his temper lest he be overwhelmed by rising hysteria. Therefore he looks for any excuse to convince himself that what he sees with his own eyes, hears with his own ears, is not true. But the sight of Kent in the stocks, reminding him of an intentional insult to himself, keeps reviving his anger; and he returns over and over to the same question: "Death on my state! Wherefore/ Should he sit here?" "Who put my man i' th' stocks?" "Who stock'd my servant?" (ll. 113-14, 185, 191).

After the entry of Goneril (l. 191), whom he greets with a question ("Art not asham'd to look upon this beard?"), and the shocking sight of Regan's welcome to her ("O Regan, wilt thou take her by the hand?"), the sisters in a turnabout take over the questioning, and by its means conduct a plausible but disingenuous argument that would reduce him to complete dependency on them. Harping on his dotage and telling him Goneril knows what she does in cutting his train in half, Regan begins:

> What, fifty followers?
> Is it not well? What should you need of more?
> Yea, or so many, sith that both charge and danger
> Speak 'gainst so great a number? How in one house

(II, iv, 240-
45)

> Should many people, under two commands,
> Hold amity? 'Tis hard; almost impossible.

Goneril warms to the argument:

Why might not you, my lord, receive attendance
From those that she calls servants, or from mine? *(II, iv, 246-47)*

And Regan chimes in with her amen: "Why not, my lord? "
When she tells him that she will allow him no more than
twenty-five, he decides he must make the hard choice of returning with Goneril, whose allowance of fifty means to him
that she has twice Regan's love. But Goneril resumes the questions with greater eloquence and greater speciousness:

Hear me, my lord.
What need you five-and-twenty, ten, or five,
To follow in a house where twice so many *(II, iv, 263-*
Have a command to tend you? *66)*

Regan moves the argument to its inevitable end: "What need
one? " This brings Lear's protesting cry, "O reason not the
need! " and with it his penetrating insight into distinctively
human needs; man lives on a purely animal level if he seeks no
more than the base satisfaction of physical needs.

Our basest beggars
Are in the poorest thing superfluous.
Allow not nature more than nature needs,
Man's life is cheap as beast's. Thou art a lady:
If only to go warm were gorgeous,
Why, nature needs not what thou gorgeous wear'st, *(II, iv, 267-*
Which scarcely keeps thee warm. *73)*

Decorum, ceremony, courtesy, elegance—things which give dignity and beauty to life—come only when man is able to live
beyond his animal needs. Civilized man does not live by bread
only. This is the first wise speech of Lear, the first in which he
moves out beyond himself in the utterance of a general truth.
But what he most needs at this moment is patience:

But for true need *(II, iv, 273-*
You heavens, give me that patience, patience I need! *74)*

and he pitifully asks the gods to touch him with noble anger,
not to let "women's weapons, water drops," stain his man's
cheeks. As he goes out into the rising storm, he makes a threat
of vengeance. We hear the same syntax we have heard before,

but this time his imagination falters. The future of strong determination is the same in form, but is now empty of content:

> No, you unnatural hags!
> I will have such revenges on you both
> That all the world shall—I will do such things—

*(II, iv, 281-
85)*

> What they are yet, I know not; but they shall be
> The terrors of the earth!

Defiance replaces command; he is threatening only to himself:

> You think I'll weep.
> No, I'll not weep.
> I have full cause of weeping, but this heart

*(II, iv, 285-
89)*

> Shall break into a hundred thousand flaws
> Or ere I'll weep. O fool, I shall go mad!

The scene ends with Regan's command to Gloucester, "Shut
up your doors," and with Cornwall's echo of it in remorseless
finality:

*(II, iv, 311-
12)*

> Shut up your doors, my lord; 'tis a wild night.
> My Regan counsels well. Come out o' th' storm.

Gloucester has no authority in his own house. Power has fully
passed to the cruel and the wicked.

   Out in the storm (III, ii, iv) Lear "Strives in his little world
of man to outscorn/ The to-and-fro-conflicting wind and rain"
(III, i, 10-11). The imperatives of petition and of command are
indistinguishable in form, almost as if he could himself command the elements:

> Blow, winds, and crack your cheeks! rage! blow!
> You cataracts and hurricanoes, spout
> Till you have drench'd our steeples, drown'd the cocks!
> You sulph'rous and thought-executing fires,
> Vaunt-couriers to oak-cleaving thunderbolts,

(III, ii, 1-6)

> Singe my white head!

Still, he knows that in his helplessness he is at their mercy—
"Here I stand your slave"—and protests the injustice of their
attack on him:

> But yet I call you servile ministers,
> That will with two pernicious daughters join

Your high-engender'd battles 'gainst a head
So old and white as this!   *(III, ii, 21-24)*

And again:

       Let the great gods,
That keep this dreadful pudder o'er our heads,
Find out their enemies now.   *(III, ii, 49-51)*

Their true enemies are those whose covert crimes are undi-
vulged and unwhipped of justice, the perjured, the concealers
of evil hearts like his daughters, the simulars of virtue. They
are the ones to "cry/ These dreadful summoners grace." He,
Lear, is "a man/ More sinn'd against than sinning." This is a
truth indeed, for his faults were vanity, not hypocrisy; the
anger of hurt pride, not malice.

    Lear's widening vision of the nature of evil, a vision so
bitter that he prays even for the destruction of mankind—

        thou, all-shaking thunder,
Strike flat the thick rotundity o' th' world,
Crack Nature's moulds, all germains spill[14] at once,
That make ingrateful man—   *(III, ii, 6-9)*

includes also a new awareness of suffering:

Poor naked wretches, whereso'er you are,
That bide the pelting of this pitiless storm,
How shall your houseless heads and unfed sides,
Your loop'd and window'd raggedness, defend you
From seasons such as these? O, I have ta'en
Too little care of this! Take physic, pomp;
Expose thyself to feel what wretches feel,
That thou mayst shake the superflux to them
And show the heavens more just.   *(III, iv, 28-36)*

Question, assertion, and command are all there, but altogether
different in emphasis and direction from anything we have
heard before. The question, even though it can be asked only
because of Lear's own immediate experience in the storm, is
not centered in himself; it is not a demand for an answer, not
an angry exclamation, not even an expression of bewilderment

14. *Germains*, that is, germens, seeds; *spill*, destroy.

as to who he is, but a question of genuine humanitarian concern: How are the unfed, the unclothed, the homeless, to endure seasons such as these? The assertion, "I have ta'en too
little care of this," is a simple admission of his own negligence
and irresponsibility. The command, "Take physic, pomp," is
addressed to rulers in general, not merely to himself.

But this high pitch, whether of prayers to the elements or
of solemn adjurations to himself, is not sustained. His three
principal sentence patterns, his three "themes," are modulated
into another key, with a new note of tenderness. When Kent
would lead him to shelter from the storm in a hovel he has
found, Lear thinks first of his Fool:

Come on, my boy. How dost, my boy? Art cold?
I am cold myself. Where is this straw, my fellow?
The art of our necessities is strange,
That can make vile things precious. Come, your hovel.
Poor fool and knave, I have one part in my heart
(III, ii, 68-73) That's sorry yet for thee.

Lear is discovering who he is. Between his speeches we have
been hearing the Fool's wry and pitiful "sentences": "O
nuncle, court holy water in a dry house is better than this rain
water out o' door" (III, ii, 10-11); "He that has a house to put
's head in has a good headpiece" (ll. 25-26). To his melancholy song on the way of the world—

He that has and a little tiny wit—
     With a hey, ho, the wind and the rain—
Must make content with his fortunes fit,
(III, ii, 74-77)   For the rain it raineth every day—

Lear assents: "True, my good boy. Come, bring us to this
hovel."

During the two storm scenes Lear's new perceptions are
interrupted by the realization of his helplessness as "A poor,
infirm, weak, and despis'd old man" and by his struggle for
self-control:

          Filial ingratitude!
Is it not as this mouth should tear this hand
For lifting food to't? But I will punish home!
No, I will weep no more. In such a night

To shut me out! Pour on; I will endure.
In such a night as this! O Regan, Goneril!
Your old kind father, whose frank heart gave all!
O, that way madness lies; let me shun that!
No more of that. *(III, iv, 14-22)*

Note again the incredulous questions, the exclamations, the declarations of future intent; but now they oscillate between shock and defiance, or between shock and the impulse to weep. The sight of Edgar as poor mad Tom, who is routed out of the hovel (l. 46), is all that is needed to end the King's slender hold on sanity. His questions take a sudden, irrational turn which yet marks his fixation:

Hast thou given all to thy two daughters, and art thou come to this? *(III, iv, 49-50)*

What, have his daughters brought him to this pass?
Couldst thou save nothing? Didst thou give 'em all? *(III, iv, 66-67)*

These questions lead to the next:

Is it the fashion that discarded fathers
Should have thus little mercy on their flesh?
Judicious punishment! 'Twas this flesh begot
Those pelican daughters. *(III, iv, 74-77)*

Poor Tom now becomes to Lear the source of wisdom, a learned Theban, from whom he can learn the secrets of the universe: "What is the cause of thunder?" He is fascinated with this Tom o' Bedlam—in rags, houseless, reduced to drinking "the green mantle of the standing pool"; to eating "the swimming frog, the toad, the tadpole, the wall-newt," and "cow-dung for sallets"; possessed by fiends who have "laid knives under his pillow and halters in his pew" (that is, who have tempted him to suicide).

Contemplation of Edgar's state leads Lear to his central question and to his observation, categorically stated, on the nature of man himself:

Why, thou wert better in thy grave than to answer with thy uncover'd body this extremity of the skies. Is man no more than this? Consider him well. Thou ow'st the worm no silk, the beast no hide, the sheep no wool, the cat no perfume. Ha!

Here's three on's are sophisticated! Thou art the thing itself;
unaccommodated man is no more but such a poor, bare, fork-
(III, iv, 105- ed animal as thou art. Off, off, you lendings! Come, unbutton
14) here.

The command is to his companions to help him off with his
clothes. This speech is at the nadir of Lear's experience; he
thinks he has discovered what man truly is in himself, and that
he must therefore reduce himself to this essential state.
Clothes are taken as the symbols of corrupt, civilized man; they
are mere borrowings, sophistications of nature, and must
therefore be discarded. We remember, however, Lear's earlier
intuition in the "O reason not the need" speech. There he had
said, "Allow not nature more than nature needs,/ Man's life is
cheap as beast's." It is indeed! Is, then, this unaccommodated
state a desirable state to return to? He did not think so then,
when he was sane. And is Tom, eating "the old rat and the
ditch-dog," the thing itself? Is man no more than a poor, bare,
forked animal? The implications of the assertion are ambiguous.
It may be well to remember who this "poor Tom" is in himself.
He is Gloucester's son, a victim of his brother's ambition and
his father's credulity, yet the one whose selfless love will save
his father. "Is man no more than this?" is the great central
question of the play. If it is answered, as I believe it is, it is
answered not explicitly, but implicitly, in the characters—the
loving as well as the hating ones—and in the experiences of
Lear and of Gloucester, that is to say, in the tragic action
itself.
    After Lear's descent into madness and his spiriting away by
Kent to Dover, it is Gloucester's turn to find the truth by
suffering and to be rescued by his outcast son Edgar, the same
Poor Tom who prompted Lear's crucial question. Like Lear,
Gloucester suffers the shock of confrontation with the ugly
truth, but the admission of his mistake is swifter, the disillu-
sion more sudden and savage. In the scene (III, vii) in which
Cornwall and Regan question him for his knowledge of the
landing of Cordelia with an army and his part in the escape of
the King, questions are put to a new use—the use of brutal
interrogation, not to find out the truth, but to force the answers the questioners want. When he tries to reply that he has
a letter from one of neutral heart, they deny his answer and

close in on him with antiphonal insistence:

Corn:	Cunning.
Reg:	And false.

Corn: Where hast thou sent the King?
Glou: To Dover.
Reg: Wherefore to Dover? Wast thou not charg'd at peril—
Corn: Wherefore to Dover? Let him first answer that.
Glou: I am tied to th' stake, and I must stand the course.
Reg: Wherefore to Dover, sir?

(III, vii, 49-55)

His courageous answer that he would not see Regan's cruel nails pluck out Lear's poor old eyes brings on him his own blinding. He is told that Edmund, on whom he calls for help, was his betrayer, and is "thrust out at gates" that he may "smell his way to Dover." This is Regan's order. Cornwall adds, "Turn out that eyeless villain." Under the new rule, questions are instruments of terror and commands are the orders of naked power.

We last saw Lear being taken in a litter to Dover, where Cordelia awaited him. But somewhere along the way he escaped from his caretakers to wander alone. Shakespeare now brings him and Gloucester, the madman and the blind man, together on the heath (IV, vi, 79ff.). Lear, again feeling himself "every inch a king" and with the old authority in his voice, preaches to Gloucester on the evil state of the world, a world Gloucester, in his blindness, sees now only "feelingly." This state has been partially exemplified in the actions of the evil characters, but here it is put in general and more inclusive terms; the episode has, therefore, a somewhat choric quality. At moments Lear imagines himself, the king, to be acting as a chief magistrate; he exercises his power on the bench absolutely and cynically. The questions he asks are cynical questions: "See how yond justice rails upon yond simple thief. . . . Change places and, handy-dandy, which is the justice, which is the thief?" (ll. 155-58). The questions are answered with cynical commands, and the commands are defended by cynical assertions of the ubiquity of lust, cupidity, hypocrisy, and injustice, as in these sequences:

When I do stare, see how the subject quakes.
I pardon that man's life. What was thy cause?

Adultery?
Thou shalt not die. Die for adultery? No.
The wren goes to't, and the small gilded fly
Does lecher in my sight.
Let copulation thrive; for Gloucester's bastard son
(IV, vi, 110- Was kinder to his father than my daughters
18) Got 'tween the lawful sheets.

Or this one, in which the assertions are more sententiously
put:

Thou rascal beadle, hold thy bloody hand!
Why dost thou lash that whore? Strip thine own back.
Thou hotly lusts to use her in that kind
For which thou whip'st her. The usurer hangs the cozener.
Through tatter'd clothes small vices do appear;
Robes and furr'd gowns hide all. Plate sin with gold,
(IV, vi, 164- And the strong lance of justice hurtless breaks;
71) Arm it in rags, a pygmy's straw does pierce it.

This sequence ends with a general pardon:

None does offend, none—I say none! I'll able 'em.
(IV, vi, 172- Take that of me, my friend, who have the power
74) To seal th' accuser's lips.

Since all offend, judged and judge alike, none offends. In place
of justice, corruption in the court; in place of responsible authority, naked power. He ends his preaching to Gloucester
with a counsel of patience drawn from ancient commonplaces
on this vale of tears:

Thou must be patient. We came crying hither;
(IV, vi, 182- Thou know'st, the first time that we smell the air
84) We wawl and cry.

And why do we?

(IV, vi, 186- When we are born, we cry that we are come
88) To this great stage of fools.

I said that this devastating vision of a corrupt world—a
world in which women are centaurs, "a dog's obey'd in office," and "robes and furr'd gowns hide all"—was choric in a
way, extending as it does beyond anything Lear is shown to
have experienced directly. But it is not the whole truth of the

world of the play. Gloucester's bastard son, we know, was not kinder to his father than Lear's elder daughters "got 'tween the lawful sheets." And there beside the two old men stands Edgar, still unrecognized, the slandered and outcast son, who has saved his father from suicide and despair. His own comment on the meeting of the madman and the blind man is a truly choric one: "I would not take this from report. It is,/ And my heart breaks at it" (ll. 144-45). In the next scene (IV, vii), Lear is to come back to sanity under the ministration of Edgar's counterpart, Cordelia.

This is, above all, a quiet scene, unadorned, and without heightening of any sort. The imperious voice is gone. As the King wakes after his long, restorative sleep (l. 42), the first questions are Cordelia's tender, courteous ones, delicately restoring a right relation to him of both love and reverence: "How does my royal lord? How fares your Majesty?" The returning pain of consciousness makes him protest:

> You do me wrong to take me out o' th' grave.
> Thou art a soul in bliss; but I am bound
> Upon a wheel of fire, that mine own tears   *(IV, vii, 45-*
> Do scald like molten lead.   *48)*

Lear's questions are of bewilderment at where he is: "You are a spirit, I know. When did you die? "; of pitiful uncertainty at his own pathetic state:

> Where have I been? Where am I? Fair daylight?   *(IV, vii, 52-*
> I am mightily abus'd;   *53)*

and of unbelieving wonder at a sight he fears cannot be true:

> *Lear:*   Do not laugh at me;
>   For (as I am a man) I think this lady
>   To be my child Cordelia.
> *Cor:*   And so I am, I am.   *(IV, vii, 68-*
> *Lear:* Be your tears wet? Yes, faith. I pray weep not.   *71)*

"Be your tears wet?" is the old incredulous question—"So young and so untender?"—reversed, and in a new key, not of anger but of wonder and hope. The answer to the riddle of Cordelia's loving according to her bond is at hand. Lear prepares himself for the worst and makes his confession:

                                              I pray weep not.
                        If you have poison for me, I will drink it.
                        I know you do not love me; for your sisters
(IV, vii. 71-   Have, as I do remember, done me wrong.
75)   You have some cause, they have not.

The conditional sentence, "If you have poison for me, I will drink it," may remind us of the love test, when it was Lear who set the condition: "What can you say to draw/ A third more opulent than your sisters?"—that is, if you say you love me best, I shall give you the richest part of my kingdom. The condition he now imagines is again quid pro quo, but with the situation reversed, and the consequence of acceptance not reward but punishment. The terms are strictly just, but quite as impossible to Cordelia as were the first. Her reply to his "You have some cause, they have not," is simply, "No cause, no cause." No conditions, no contingencies, no quantities. Lear's last words in the scene are a simple petition and a simple assertion.

(IV, vii, 83-   You must bear with me.
84)   Pray you now, forget and forgive. I am old and foolish.

Recognition and acceptance are complete.

The last three scenes of the play (V, i, ii, iii) are given over to the complicated denouement, in which the British defeat the French invaders; Lear and Cordelia are captured and sent to prison; the evil sisters destroy each other; Edmund is mortally wounded by his brother Edgar in a formal trial by combat; Kent and Edgar, who have stood faithfully by master and father, are recognized and recount their own pilgrimages. It seems as if right and justice, under Albany, will prevail after all. But before the combat Edmund had ordered the deaths of Lear and Cordelia in prison, and his countermanding order, made when he was about to die himself, comes too late. Before the two went off to prison (V, iii, 26), we had heard Lear's idyllic vision of his reunion with Cordelia:

                        Come, let's away to prison.
                        We two will sing like birds i' th' cage.
                        When thou dost ask me blessing, I'll kneel down
(V, iii, 8-11)   And ask of thee forgiveness;

and we had heard his happy renunciation of sublunary and transitory power:

> we'll wear out
> In a wall'd prison, packs and sects of great ones
> That ebb and flow by th' moon.   *(V, iii, 17-19)*

Now we are to see Lear return with Cordelia dead in his arms:

> Howl, howl, howl, howl! O, you are men of stone.
> . . . She's gone for ever!
> I know when one is dead, and when one lives.   *(V, iii, 257-*
> She's dead as earth.   *61)*

The old Lear is not gone: he shows again the mighty grief, the rage which gave him strength to kill Cordelia's hangman, the impatience when the others close around him: "A plague upon you, murderers, traitors all!/ I might have sav'd her; now she's gone for ever!"

He phrases two conditional sentences—as we have seen, a form not common with him:

> Lend me a looking glass.
> If that her breath will mist or stain the stone,   *(V, iii, 261-*
> Why, then she lives.   *63)*

The second follows from the first.

> This feather stirs; she lives! If it be so,
> It is a chance which does redeem all sorrows   *(V, iii, 265-*
> That ever I have felt.   *67)*

The sight moves Kent, Albany, and Edgar to speak chorically, in question and petition:

> *Kent:*   Is this the promis'd end?
> *Edg:* Or image of that horror?   *(V, iii, 263-*
> *Alb:*   Fall and cease.   *64)*

Does the immensity of this horror prefigure even the Day of Judgment? For pity's sake, let the end come.

Now Albany makes a solemn declaration of intent, a promise which is like a command, to restore justice and order:

> All friends shall taste
> The wages of their virtue, and all foes   *(V, iii, 302-*
> The cup of their deservings.   *4)*

All friends? Cutting into this promise comes Lear's protesting, heartbroken, unanswerable question, his last one, on the ulti- mate injustice of Cordelia's death:

Why should a dog, a horse, a rat have life,
(V, iii, 305-6) And thou no breath at all?

Her breath has not stained the stone, his sorrows will not be redeemed.

Thou'lt come no more.
Never, never, never, never, never.
Pray you undo this button. Thank you, sir.
(V, iii, 306- Do you see this? Look on her! look! her lips!
11) Look there, look there!

He dies in the illusion that she is coming back to life. The three modes of command, question, and assertion which opened the play—the three themes, if we return to our musical metaphor—have been brought to a close in Lear's own voice.

The final speech of the play, Albany's, is a simple statement of the magnitude of the tragedy. This statement is without a command, without a question, without a sententious assertion, without a declaration, even, of future intent:

The weight of this sad time we must obey,
Speak what we feel, not what we ought to say.
(V, iii, 323- The oldest have borne most; we that are young
26) Shall never see so much, nor live so long.

Antony and Cleopatra: 4
The Stillness and the Dance
MAYNARD MACK

I

Antony and Cleopatra is the delight of audiences and the despair of critics. Its delight for audiences springs, in part at
least, from its being inexhaustible to contemplation, as Coleridge implies when he speaks of its "angelic strength," the
"happy valiancy" of its style, and calls it of all Shakespeare's
plays "the most wonderful." No doubt its delight for today's
audiences owes something also to its being the most accessible
of the major Shakespearean tragedies to twentieth-century
sensibilities, especially those not much experienced in drama
apart from that of the realistic stage. There are no witches in
Antony and Cleopatra to require a mild suspension of disbe-
lief, no ghosts, no antic madmen, no personages who are para-
gons of good or evil, nor even any passions (such, for example,
as Coriolanus's contempt for the Roman commoners) which
require of today's spectator an act of imaginative adjustment.
True, the play's story of the ruin of a great man by an enchantress (if that *is* its story) must have carried more plausibility in 1607 than it does today, when our enchantresses, mini-
skirted and twiggy, seem unlikely to endanger anyone who has
got past his freshman year, and our great men are in depress-
ingly short supply. Nonetheless, the enchantment formula has

The occasion on which this lecture was delivered was a particularly
happy one for me, and I want to thank particularly Milton Crane,
George McCandlish, Calvin Linton, and Stephen Brown for the generous part they took in making it so.

In printing the lecture, quotations and line numbers have been re-
vised to accord with the text established in the *Complete Pelican
Shakespeare,* ed. Alfred Harbage, collected ed. (Baltimore: Penguin
Books Inc., 1969).

the virtue of being familiar to us, however shrunken the
modern instances (some of us will here remember the Profumo
case), and it has, besides, for those who insist on realism, the
sanction of history, or at least such history as Plutarch,
Appian, and Lucius Florus knew how to write. I suppose it
has, too, the sanction of what a present fashion likes to call
our fantasy-life. There is no woman, one may be permitted to
believe, who has not somewhere in her being a touch, or
twitch, of Cleopatra; no man who has not entertained, at some
time, the dream of exercising a magnanimity like Antony's,
setting his beloved in a hail of barbaric pearl and gold, dis-
posing of men and measures with an imperious nod, and
falling, if fall he must, with a panache that makes women weep
and strong men suck in their waistlines. Even the Victorian
lady who is reported to have whispered to her husband at the
close of a performance of *Antony and Cleopatra*, "How unlike
the home-life of our own dear Queen!" may be presumed to
have lingered a little longer than usual over her toilette the next
day.

II

So much for audiences. For critics, as I have said, the case is
different. If the play is inexhaustible to contemplation, it is at
the same time remarkably inaccessible to interpretation, or at
any rate to a consensus of interpretation, as the critical record
shows. There seems to be a delicacy combined with intricacy
in the play's interior balance that no criticism can lay hold of
for long without oversimplifying or oversetting, including the
criticism speculatively offered here. Magnanimous emperor,
calculating politician, charismatic leader, reckless lover and
risk-taker, posturer, angry husband—all these figures are contained in Antony, yet he is not reducible to any of them or
even to all together. Cleopatra is actress, trickster, trull, and
loving wife; she is "wrinkled deep in time" yet timeless, "East-
ern star" and "morsel, cold upon Dead Caesar's trencher,"
"Royal Egypt" but "commanded By such poor passion as the
maid that milks And does the meanest chares." Yet relevant
as these categories are in her case too, she manages to escape
them, as the widely disparate estimates of her conduct made

by spectators as well as readers show. Even at the play's end, there remains a sense in which, as the 116th sonnet says of another "star," her "worth's unknown, although [her] height be taken."

The play, moreover, like the lovers, makes no confidences. Soliloquies and asides, though engaged in by Enobarbus, are evidently foreign to Shakespeare's conception of heroic character in this play, or at least to his conception of the optimum relation between these protagonists and us. We are never brought close to them by a secret shared, a motive, conscious or unconscious, suddenly divulged. We watch them always from a distance, uncertain how far to accept their actions—and which actions—at face value, how far to believe the commentary of the observers in which Shakespeare again and again frames them, and even how to reconcile one action with the next. Antony is never allowed for an instant to reflect for our benefit on his betrayal of Cleopatra in marrying Octavia or on his betrayal of Octavia and Caesar in returning to Cleopatra or, as we might perhaps especially expect, on the meaning of his past experiences as he dies. We learn only that he lived "the greatest prince o' th' world, The noblest" (a summary which considerably begs the question), and dies now, not basely or cowardly in surrender to Caesar, but by his own hand, "a Roman, by a Roman Valiantly vanquished" (IV, xv, 54 ff.). As for Cleopatra, Enobarbus tells us what *he* makes of her cajoleries with Thidias, and he is in some sense our guide:

Antony: Sir, sir, thou art so leaky
That we must leave thee to thy sinking, for
Thy dearest quit thee.

(III, xiii, 63-65)

Yet this episode is followed by one of the most endearing reconciliation scenes ever written, one in which I see no shred of evidence to show that Cleopatra is lying and Antony her dupe:

Antony: Alack, our terrene moon
Is now eclipsed, and it portends alone
The fall of Antony!
Cleopatra: I must stay his time.
Antony: To flatter Caesar, would you mingle eyes
With one that ties his points?
Cleopatra: Not know me yet?

Antony: Cold-hearted toward me?
Cleopatra: Ah, dear, if I be so,
   From my cold heart let heaven engender hail,
   And poison it in the source, and the first stone
   Drop in my neck: as it determines, so
   Dissolve my life! The next Caesarion smite,
   Till by degrees the memory of my womb,
   Together with my brave Egyptians all,
   By the discandying of this pelleted storm,
   Lie graveless, till the flies and gnats of Nile
(III, xiii, 153-   Have buried them for prey!
67)   *Antony:*   I am satisfied.

    Antony is satisfied, but critics understandably have not
been. For if this expresses her real feelings, what was she up to
with Thidias, and what did the playwright wish us to make of
Enobarbus's remark about the leaky ship? On the other hand,
if these lines must be dismissed as rhetoric, so must almost
every other expression of emotion in the play, for they are all
of a hyperbolic piece, including Cleopatra's grief at Antony's
death and her dream of him recounted to Dolabella. Similar
questions, we realize, haunt our impressions of her interview
with Caesar, when her treasurer either gives her game away or
affects to, and also of the two failures of her ships at Actium.
Why, at that first battle, does she fly? Is it simple fear ("Forgive my fearful sails" [III, xi, 55])? Or does her woman's intuition suspect that the ultimate contest against Caesar is already
lost? Or that a victory for Antony would be a defeat for her,
since in that event he might be struck again by that "Roman
thought" which earlier deprived her of him? Or is it perhaps
her hope, by taking herself out of the battle, to strengthen her
negotiating position, no matter to whom the victory falls? The
second occasion is yet more puzzling. This time the fleet not
only yields to the foe, but "yonder They cast their caps up,
and carouse together Like friends long lost," and Antony's
inference from this that he has been "betrayed" by Cleopatra,
"Beguiled . . . to the very heart of loss" (IV, xii, 11 ff.), seems
unexceptionable. How else to account for a surrender without
(apparently) a single blow struck? Yet Cleopatra's emissary,
Diomedes, later tells Antony and us that no such treason occurred, at least none in which she had a hand:

> for when she saw
> (Which never shall be found) you did suspect
> She had disposed with Caesar, and that your rage
> Would not be purged, she sent you word she was dead.
>
> *(IV, xiv, 121-24)*

I labor the obvious in these instances because I believe that Shakespeare means us to take note of what he is about. I cannot persuade myself, as some recent critics have done, that his failure to supply "the directives to the audience that are obviously needed" springs from inattention or fatigue, the play being so clearly in all other respects the product of a poetic consciousness supremely alert, and even, I would wish to add, rather plainly disposed to jolt us from our usual automatisms and stock responses. For what else can be the intent of that unusual structure, already mentioned, whereby every major action of the lovers is enveloped in a choral commentary that we are simultaneously aware does not quite adequately represent it? What else can be the intent of establishing so many wide polarities—Rome and Egypt, nature and art, war and love, indulgence and austerity, loyalty and self-interest, sincerity and affectation, and many others—and of so steadfastly refusing to resolve them or adjudicate between them? Even a great deal of the play's language seems calculated to question or explode our habitual safe norms and logical expectations; for it bristles with startling oxymorons, contradictions, and abrupt reversals that every playgoer will recall: the bellows that cools, not kindles (I, i, 9); the fans that heat the cheek they cool "And what they undid did" (II, ii, 203-5); the woman "wrinkled deep in time" (I, v, 29), whom age, however, cannot wither, who makes "defect perfection," and, when breathless, "power breathe[s] forth" (II, ii, 231-33); the man who can say "with a wound I must be cured" (IV, xiv, 78) and whose bounty "grew the more by reaping" (V, ii, 86-88); the prayer that prays and yet unprays itself—"Husband win, win brother, Prays, and destroys the prayer" (III, iv, 18-19); our "most persisted deeds" that yet "compel" us to lament them (V, i, 29-30); the "lover's pinch, Which hurts, and is desir'd" (V, ii, 294-95); the asp that is both death and lover, or death and infant, or possibly all three (V, ii, 243 ff.).

Again, I stress the obvious. What these effects convey is the same intricate balance of opposing impulses and conflicting attitudes that characterize the play throughout. Somewhere dimly behind them we may sense not only the playwright's effort to achieve a style that will accommodate the story he has to tell in its extremes of grandeur and folly, dignity and humiliation, but, just possibly, the mood of serious play (I suspect this is among the meanings Coleridge meant to assign to his "happy valiancy") that seems to shine out in all Renaissance works that draw heavily on the vein of paradox. Not impossibly, Shakespeare was himself conscious of his propinquity in this instance to that honorable tradition. With a heroine who was historically guaranteed both whore and queen, yet who, in popular story, had additionally been looked on as an exemplar of fidelity, one of love's own martyrs; with a hero, too, who was credited with being one of the greatest soldiers in the world and at the same time one of the greatest lovers and revelers; and with a source, or a set of sources, certain to attract a poet's mind toward the ancient question whether the world can ever be well lost, and if so, for what return, Shakespeare must have been considerably less clairvoyant about the implications of his materials than he usually shows himself to be if he did not see that in *Antony and Cleopatra* he was engaged in the central act of the paradoxist, which is to defend the indefensible, or at least to defend something which is widely held to be indefensible, like Erasmus's "Folly" or Donne's "Inconstancy in Women." Plato's Gorgias, we are told, set himself the paradoxical task of praising Helen, who had brought ruin by her adulterous beauty to all Greece, and succeeded so well at it that his successors supposed he had been serious and took her thereafter for a proper object of praise. It was not the last time that this would happen. Milton's effort to lift Satan, who had brought ruin to all mankind, out of the category of common bugaboo and fiend (a spectacular exercise in defending the indefensible), was to enjoy, after an interval, a similar success in certain quarters, as was Swift's praise of stoic apathy in the fourth book of *Gulliver*. We know far less of course of Shakespeare's intentions because we know far less of him. But whatever they were, it is safe to say that he has left us a pair of reckless and irresponsible lovers so well praised that audience and critic alike still find it impossible to sort out their sympathies. In other words, the paradox of his theme, whether he himself saw it or not, continues to "do his kind," as the clown says of the worm (V, ii, 262): it continues to be faithful to the nature of paradox, which is "to be paradoxical, to do two things at once, two things which contradict . . . one another."[1]

III

Considered as pure story, the play that Shakespeare makes of Antony and Cleopatra would have delighted Chaucer's Monk. For it obviously owes much, at least in its general outline, to the medieval tragic formula of the fall-of-princes and mirror-for-magistrates tradition, which the Monk enunciates to the Canterbury pilgrims, and which was still, in 1607, owing to a good deal of Elizabethan dramatic practice including Shakespeare's own, far better known than Plutarch to playhouse audiences. Tragedy, according to this formula, is what happens when eminent historical personages lose their foothold on the pinnacle of wealth or power and plummet down to ruin with a gratifying homiletic crash. Implied in Plutarch's narrative inevitably, though only desultorily stressed there and sometimes lost in masses of detail better suited to biography than to homily, the theme of lost (or gained) imperium became for Shakespeare the central issue.

For this reason, his Antony is brought before us at the zenith of his eminence, when his soldiership ("twice the other twain," says Pompey, comparing him with Lepidus and Caesar) is critically in demand. He already holds the whole of

1. Rosalie Colie, *Paradoxia Epidemica* (Princeton, New Jersey: Princeton University Press, 1966), p. 8. This is a fascinating exploration of the uses of paradox in the Renaissance, to which I am here indebted. I suspect I may be indebted elsewhere in the essay (in Shakespeare criticism, *meum* and *tuum* are all but impossible to distinguish, particularly between friends) to a chapter in Miss Colie's forthcoming book on Shakespeare and to some pages by Janet Adelman soon to appear in her superb study of *Antony and Cleopatra* (New Haven, Connecticut: Yale University Press, 1973). To any other creditors whom I may have forgotten, I also express my thanks.

While this note was being prepared for publication in midsummer 1972, Miss Colie's tragic death occurred. I therefore seize the opportunity to pay tribute to an outstanding scholar and a gracious lady: *sit tibi terra levis*. Such as it is, I offer this essay to her memory.

the gorgeous East in fee and now is about to be freed from
threats, on one side by his reconciliation with Caesar and marriage to Caesar's sister; on the other, by the victories of his
lieutenant Ventidius in Parthia. He is also, we quickly learn,
about to throw all this away for the fascinating creature shown
us in four of the first five scenes and in Enobarbus's description of Cleopatra on the Cydnus. For conquest has several
forms, it seems. There is more than one kind of stronghold to
attract a soldier:

> those his goodly eyes
> That o'er the files and musters of the war
> Have glowed like plated Mars, now bend, now turn
> The office and devotion of their view

(I, i, 2-6) Upon a tawny front;

and there is more than one kind of attitude that may be taken
toward the imperium of Rome:

> Let Rome in Tiber melt and the wide arch
> Of the ranged empire fall! Here is my space,

(I, i, 33-35) Kingdoms are clay.

In short, from the moment we are introduced to Antony, we
are made aware of the undertow that will sweep him away,
and this is kept so vividly before us in every scene thereafter—
by Cleopatra, Enobarbus, Caesar, Pompey, the soothsayer, and
Antony himself—that it is only a small exaggeration to say that
Shakespeare's story of Antony's fall and of its consequences
moves from the first scene of act I to the last scene of act V
uninterruptedly, despite the presence of certain early scenes in
which, ostensibly, his political fortunes are on the rise.

The play has other features, too, that if not derived from
the medieval formula are at any rate in tune with it. Treatment
of the protagonists from the outside and from a certain aesthetic distance, so as to enhance the element of spectacle and
with it our impression that we behold a sort of paradigm or
exemplum in the *de casibus* tradition, is one such feature that
I have already underscored. So is the corollary reliance on
choric commentary rather than interior meditation to point up
the stages leading to the disaster, and particularly the emphasis
laid by this means (and in every other imaginable way) on the

grandeur of the world the protagonists inhabit and on their own special magnificence and magnanimity, in order to increase the pathos of their fall, however much that fall may be shown to be self-caused.

The play is further attuned to the formula in insisting simultaneously on what is *not* self-caused, on fortune, accident, destiny, doom—all that in the original medieval context might have been called the will of God and here is hinted at least to be the will of one god: "'Tis the god Hercules, whom Antony loved, Now leaves him" (IV, iii, 15-16). Shakespeare may have been moved to this equivocal management by a bemusing sentence in his source. For Plutarch says of Cleopatra's plea to be allowed to join the wars against Caesar (in Plutarch's narrative, delivered to Antony through a bribed Canidius): "These fair persuasions won him; for it was predestined that the government of all the world should fall into Octavius Caesar's hands." Hence it was Antony's decision, except that it was also destiny's. Just so, in the play, though our attention is repeatedly called to Antony's misjudgments, a sense of impersonal fate runs deep. Caesar, as Bradley says, is "the Man of Destiny, the agent of forces against which the intentions of an individual could avail nothing," one from whom "the feeling of fate comes through to us."[2] The language repeatedly proclaims this. Whereas "noble" is the play's characterizing term for Antony (despite his sometimes ignoble deeds like the whipping of Thidias), Caesar's characterizing term is "fortune." This word, with its cognates and synonyms, appears some forty times in *Antony and Cleopatra*, more than twice as often as in any other of the major tragedies, and repeatedly in connection with Caesar, whose invisible "genius" it appears to be. Antony's own genius, the soothsayer assures him immediately after his marriage to Octavia, "is Noble, courageous, high, unmatchable," but placed near Caesar's it is overpowered; "and of that natural luck, He beats thee 'gainst the odds" (II, iii, 19 ff.). From that point on, Caesar regularly beats Antony against the odds, and is spoken of increasingly as "fortunate Caesar" (IV, xiv, 76), "full-fortuned Caesar" (IV, xv, 24), the man whom Antony has to address after Actium as

2. A. C. Bradley, *Oxford Lectures on Poetry* (Oxford: The Clarendon Press, 1909), p. 290.

"Lord of his fortunes" (III, xii, 11), and the man whose "luck," we are told by Cleopatra, he learns eventually to mock: "I see him rouse himself," she says of Antony as she is dying, "To praise my noble act. I hear him mock The luck of Caesar" (V, ii, 283-85).

Something similar seems to hold true for Cleopatra. Though Antony chooses her and we are shown the familiar feminine skills with which she draws him, the play keeps alive a complementary assurance that a power works through her which is also, in some sense, a fate. She is for everyone an "enchantress," a "fairy," a "witch," a "charm," a "spell," and she moves, even for the Romans, in an ambience of suggestion that seems to give these terms a reach beyond their conventional horizons of gallantry and erotic praise. The sun makes love to her; the air, "except for vacancy," would have gone to see her triumphant landing from the Cydnus; her sighs and tears are greater storms and tempests than almanacs can report; she is cunning past man's thought; her variety is infinite; and the fetters in which she binds, like those of Merlin's Vivien, are "strong," as is also—to recall a phrase of Caesar's when he sees her in death—her "toil of grace":

> she looks like sleep,
> As she would catch another Antony
> In her strong toil of grace.

(V, ii, 344-46)

The phrase captures her mystery superbly because its range of meaning is altogether indeterminable. Is the emphasis in "toil" on the cruel snare of the hunter or on the delighting web of the accomplished woman's charms? Do the boundaries of "grace" include simply the feline movements of the experienced beast of prey, or do they extend to the worldly accomplishments cited by Claudius in giving young Laertes permission to return to Paris: "Time be thine, And thy best graces spend it at thy will," or do they glance also toward the enigmatic territories touched on by Prospero when, in praising Ariel for his simulation of the harpy, he sums up in five words the meaning of the disasters in *The Tempest* and (some critics would have it) of those in *Antony and Cleopatra* as well?

> Bravely the figure of this harpy hast thou
> Performed, my Ariel; *a grace it had, devouring.*

(III, iii, 83-84; italics mine)

My point, of course, is not that there is a right answer to these questions, but rather that the play teases us into asking them. Shakespeare's medieval inheritance remains strong enough to enable him to show us a catastrophe that Antony has quite literally made love to as if it were simultaneously a "doom."

IV

The "fall" story chiseled out of Plutarch receives in the finished play many kinds of imaginative extension, as every spectator will remember. One of these is the intricately elaborated context of mobility and mutability within which the fall is shown to occur, so that here as elsewhere in Shakespeare a play's characteristic "world" and its major action tend to become expressions of each other.

Our sense of a world in flux in *Antony and Cleopatra* is created primarily through the imagery, as many have pointed out, but in the theater it reaches us yet more directly through continual shifts of place (to mention only those of the first three acts: from Egypt to Rome to Egypt to Messina to Rome to Egypt to Misenum to Syria to Rome to Egypt to Athens to Rome to Actium to Egypt), and in the number and brevity of the episodes and scenes. In its episodic character, in fact, the play again seems mindful of the medieval past, each scene acted, as it were, from an appropriate historical "maison" or pageant-wagon, as in the cyclical plays. Today, the text of *Antony and Cleopatra* is usually divided into forty-two scenes, and while these need not be taken seriously as divisions of the action, since the folio text has neither scenes nor acts, their number indicates to us how often we are asked to register that one time, place, mood, or person gives way before another.

To this we must add the equally striking circumstance that *Antony and Cleopatra* in performance contains just under two hundred distinct entrances and exits (rather more than one per minute of playing time) and that a great many of these acquire a special impact on our senses, either from being ceremonial and accompanied by much fanfare or from their effect in bringing about emotionally significant leave-takings and reunions. People flow to and away from each other in *Antony and Cleopatra* with relentless frequency and ease—Antony from Cleopatra and to her, to Caesar and from him; Octavia from Caesar and to him, to Antony and from him; Enobarbus from Antony, then (in heart) to him; and Cleopatra—who can say? This pattern is climaxed by the great reunions and leave-takings of the close. Antony, after being reunited with Cleopatra in her monument, takes his last farewell of her ("I am dying, Egypt, dying"); Cleopatra takes hers of Caesar and the world ("Give me my robe, put on my crown"); and both farewells are preludes, so the lovers insist, to a further reunion in the Elysian fields, or on the Cydnus, where the great passion will begin anew. Nothing seems to be granted finality in *Antony and Cleopatra*, perhaps not even death.

Mobility and mutability are not confined to spatial and geographical forms, but penetrate the play at every point. They are reiterated in the allusions to the ebbing and flowing of the tides; the rising and setting (or eclipse and extinction) of stars, moons, and suns; the immense reversals of feeling in the lovers and in Enobarbus; the career of Pompey, whose powers, "crescent" in II, i, are by III, v scattered and the man himself dead; and the steady erosion of persons whom for a moment we have known or heard of as presences: Fulvia, Lepidus, Pompey, Pacorus, Enobarbus, Alexas, and Eros all are dead before Antony dies; Menas and Menecrates, Philo and Demetrius, Ventidius and Scarus have disappeared without a trace, along with Mardian; Candidus and Decretas (besides Alexas and Enobarbus) have turned their coats, and Cleopatra may or may not have been several times on the verge of turning hers.

In addition, the style itself generates impressions of this kind. Johnson's account of the play rightly emphasizes the "hurry," the "quick succession" of events that calls the attention forward; and part of the effect he has in mind comes clearly from the style, which pours rather than broods (as in *Macbeth*), which is sensuous rather than intellectual (as in *Hamlet*), and which, as Pope said of Homer's, animates everything it touches: from Philo's view of Antony in I, i, where eyes glow, bend, turn, and the heart remembers buckles it has burst in the scuffles of great fights, to Cleopatra's view of him in V, ii, where he bestrides, rears, crests; quails and shakes the orb with rattling thunder; gives in a perpetual autumn; sports like a dolphin above the ocean of his pleasure; and scatters crowns and coronets from his pockets as if they were small change.

Most striking of all, perhaps, is Shakespeare's use of the grammatical mood that, of all moods, best expresses mobility and mutability: the optative. Most of the great speeches in the play are "options"—in the radical sense. At all levels, high and low, playful and serious, hearts continually press forward with their longings, so much so that by placing even a few of them in sequence one may easily recapitulate the action.

Let Rome in Tiber melt. *(I, i, 33)*

Let me be married to three kings in a fore-
noon and widow them all. . . . Find me to marry
me with Octavius Caesar, and companion me with
my mistress. *(I, ii, 25-29)*

   Upon your sword
Sit laurel victory, and smooth success
Be strewed before your feet! *(I, iii, 99-101)*

Let his shames quickly
Drive him to Rome. *(I, iv, 72-73)*

   But all the charms of love,
Salt Cleopatra, soften thy waned lip!
Let witchcraft join with beauty, lust with both! *(II, i, 20-22)*

     Let her live
To join our kingdoms and our hearts and never
Fly off our loves again. *(II, ii, 151-53)*

Would I had never come from thence, nor you thither. *(II, iii, 12)*

Melt Egypt into Nile! and kindly creatures
Turn all to serpents! *(II, v, 78-79)*

In thy fats our cares be drowned,
With thy grapes our hairs be crowned. *(II, vii, 114-15)*

   Sink Rome, and their tongues rot
That speak against us! *(III, vii, 15-16)*

   O that I were
Upon the hill of Basan, to outroar
The hornèd herd! *(III, xiii, 126-28)*

This is a selection simply, and from the first three acts. Thereafter, for obvious reasons, the optative mood quickens, to cul-
minate at last in three of the best known utterances in the
play:

We'll bury him; and then, what's brave, what's noble,
(IV, xv, 89- Let's do't after the high Roman fashion,
91) And make death proud to take us.

I dreamt there was an Emperor Antony.
O, such another sleep, that I might see
(V, ii, 76-78) But such another man!

(V, ii, 286-   Husband,I come:
87) Now to that name my courage prove my title!

To all these impressions of a world in motion, much is
added in performance by the playwright's insistent stress on
messages and messengers—though here, doubtless, other effects
and purposes must also receive their due. To ignore a man's
messenger who has a legitimate claim on you, as Antony does
in I, i, or to have such a messenger whipped, as he does in III,
xiii, or, like Cleopatra in II, v, to assault a messenger for the
bad news he carries: these are Shakespeare's equivalents in this
play of Hamlet's melancholy, Lear's quick wrath—marks of the
tragic personage's incapacity or unwillingness to adjust to the
world he lives in. Messengers also, of course, enhance our sense
of power and of the rearrangements that take place in power
as the play wears on. Cleopatra's inexhaustible supply of emis-
saries and her determination to "unpeople Egypt" (I, v, 78)
rather than let Antony in Rome go a day without a letter bear
testimony to her political stature at the outset of the play as
well as to her passion. Later on, the fact that Antony, who has
had "superfluous kings for messengers" (III, xii, 5), is reduced
to using his children's schoolmaster to carry a message to
Caesar serves as an index to the audience as well as to Caesar
that his wing has indeed been "plucked." Such effects are of
course highly visual in performance, and capable in some con-
texts of communicating exquisite ironies. In the last scene, for
instance, Caesar's messengers come and go again and again in a
fine show of strategy and efficiency, but then comes the messenger no one anticipated, a bumpkin and malapropist bearing

figs, who is escorted in by Caesar's own guard; and he proves to be the messenger that counts.

Beyond this, the play's emphasis on messengers reminds us that, in so volatile and mutable a world, opinion and report are matters of huge concern. All these people have an immense curiosity about each other, especially the Romans about Cleopatra, which they can only satisfy with fresh news. "From Alexandria," says Caesar to Lepidus the first time we see him, "This is the news" (I, iv, 3-4), and he goes on to detail Antony's ill courses there. After the triumvirs have made peace in Rome, Enobarbus is no sooner left alone with Maecenas and Agrippa than they throw out bait about life in Egypt that they hope he will rise to: "Eight wild-boars roasted whole at a breakfast, and but twelve persons there. Is this true?" says Maecenas (II, ii, 180-81). Pompey plays a like game with Antony, hinting at the time when Cleopatra kept an assignation with Julius Caesar by having herself rolled up inside a mattress and carried to him (II, vi, 68); while Lepidus, in the brawl on Pompey's galley, speculates drunkenly—but inquiringly—about pyramises and crocodiles (II, vii, 24 ff.).

This is merely the surface of "report" in the play. It soon turns out that almost everyone we meet is passionately conscious of report in other senses: not simply the public report of Rome, which Caesar is concerned as far as possible to manipulate and even Antony and Cleopatra from time to time feel the need to placate or consciously defy, but the report of history. This too is an aspect of the play that insists on its aesthetic distance from us, on its character as spectacle and exemplum. Caesar is walking into history, and is keenly conscious of it; in fact, he hopes to guarantee a good "report" for himself by composing it: "Go with me to my tent," he says to Agrippa and Maecenas, after Antony's death has been announced to him:

> where you shall see
> How hardly I was drawn into this war,
> How calm and gentle I proceeded still
> In all my writings. Go with me, and see
> What I can show in this. *(V, i, 73-77)*

Enobarbus, throughout his hesitations about leaving Antony, looks forward to what "story" will say of him if he stays—

The loyalty well held to fools does make
Our faith mere folly: yet he that can endure
To follow with allegiance a fall'n lord,
Does conquer him that did his master conquer
And earns a place i' th' story.

(III, xiii, 42-46)

—though it must be admitted he reckoned without Plutarch, who gives his going over to Caesar and his repentance short shrift, and says nothing whatever about his hesitations. Again, in his death scene, all alone, he appeals to the "blessèd moon" to bear him witness, "When men revolted shall upon record Bear hateful memory," that he repents his betrayal of his master, and then, as if resigning himself to an eternity of bad notices in the *theatrùm mundi*, concludes:

O, Antony,
Nobler than my revolt is infamous,
Forgive me in thine own particular,
But let the world rank me in register
A master leaver and a fugitive.

(IV, ix, 7 ff.)

The lovers' own consciousness of being ever on parade before the reviewing stand of world opinion is particularly acute. Antony's anguished "I have offended reputation" after Actium means more than simply that he has stained his individual honor, or even his immediate public image; he has also deviated from the world's conception of what a Roman soldier is and does, guarded and passed on from generation to generation in world opinion. When he takes Cleopatra in his arms at the play's beginning, he is conscious of the world as audience; in fact, he invokes it:

The nobleness of life
Is to do thus; when such a mutual pair
And such a twain can do't, in which I bind,
On pain of punishment, the world to weet
We stand up peerless.

(I, i, 36-40)

When he anticipates their reunion in the Elysian fields, he thinks of the audience they will have there:

Where souls do couch on flowers, we'll hand in hand,
And with our sprightly port make the ghosts gaze.

(IV, xiv, 51-52)

When Eros takes his own life rather than kill him, the thought that captivates his imagination is that Eros and Cleopatra will have won a nobler place in history than his: "My queen and Eros Have by their brave instruction got upon me A nobleness in record."

This, too, as everyone will remember, is the concern that occupies Cleopatra as she steels herself after Antony's death to do "what's brave, what's noble ... after the high Roman fashion," and so win fame, not obloquy, in the chronicles of times to come (IV, xv, 85 ff.). Her wish that her women "show" her "like a queen" in her "best attires" (V, ii, 227-28)—though no doubt partly vanity and partly calculated staginess for Caesar's last view of her—is partly too, one feels, her sense of what is suitable, in the record that will be forthcoming, "for a princess Descended of so many royal kings." Caesar's parting words about her have the quality of an epitaph, and seal the immortality in "report" that now awaits all three:

She shall be buried by her Antony.
No grave upon the earth shall clip in it
A pair so famous. High events as these
Strike those that make them; and their story is
No less in pity than his glory which
Brought them to be lamented. *(V, ii, 356-61)*

V

The imaginative extension that Shakespeare gives to the story of Antony's fall by surrounding it with a world in which, as Mutability says in *The Faerie Queene*, "Nothing doth firme and permanent appeare, But all things tost and turnèd by transverse," has its counterpart in the extension he gives the love affair. Everyone who reads or sees the play is struck at once by the hyperbolic character of the value the lovers set on each other, or at any rate the hyperbolic character of their own conception of that value: "There's beggary," as Antony puts it, "in the love that can be reckoned" (I, i, 15).

The play as a whole, supporting but also qualifying this attitude, sets moving around it an enormous traffic of evocation, primarily of two sorts. One sort moves the love affair in

the general direction of allegory and myth. In some sense, the
play hints, there looms behind Antony's choice of "Pleasure"
the great model of Hercules at the Crossroads—a popular motif
of Renaissance painting and engraving about which much has
been written by the iconographers—choosing between Virtue
and Pleasure, who are represented in two females as opposite
in their qualities as Octavia and Cleopatra, or Rome and
Egypt. It has been pointed out, too, that behind the play's
references to a great warrior feminized—Cleopatra putting her
robes on Antony, for instance, and wearing his sword Philip-
pan, or Canidius's remark after the decision to fight at Actium
by sea: "so our leader's led, And we are women's men" (III,
vii, 69-70)—may be discerned another favorite Renaissance
exemplum: Hercules's servitude in woman's dress to Omphale,
which Plutarch explicitly compares to Antony's in his *Comparison of Demetrius with Antonius*:

But to conclude, [Demetrius] neuer had ouerthrow or misfor-
tune through negligence, nor by delaying time to follow his
owne pleasure; as we see in painted tables, where *Omphale*
secretly stealeth away *Hercules* clubbe, and took his Lyon
skinne from him: euen so *Cleopatra* oftentimes vnarmed *Antonius*, and enticed him to her, making him lose matters of great
importance, and very needfull iournies, to come and be
dandled with her.[3]

To these the play adds two further analogies, Aeneas and
Dido, and Mars and Venus, whose implications are far less
clear. Though at first Antony might be said to imitate Aeneas
in abandoning his Dido for a Roman destiny and a Latin marriage, his later career substantively revises the Virgilian story in
that he abandons Rome and empire for his African queen and,
in the only overt allusion the play makes to Virgil's lovers,
anticipates that he and Cleopatra in the afterworld will be
admired more than they for their eminence in love: "Dido and
her Aeneas shall want troops, And all the haunt be ours" (IV,
xiv, 53-54). Does Shakespeare nod here, forgetting Virgil's

3. I owe this passage to the illuminating chapter on *Antony and
Cleopatra* in Ernest Schanzer's *Problem Plays of Shakespeare* (New
York: Schocken Books, 1963), which also discusses, with an emphasis
quite different from mine, the analogies to Hercules, Aeneas, and Mars.

own depiction in book VI of the estrangement of Dido from
Aeneas on his visit to the underworld? Or is this simply Antony's exuberant imagination undertaking to bring reality closer
to the heart's desire, as he does so often elsewhere? Or does
Shakespeare, for whatever reasons, choose to see Aeneas in the
Chaucerian and generally medieval perspectives that had already made of Dido, as of Cleopatra, an exemplar of faithful
love?

Similar questions must be asked about the playwright's as-
sociation of his lovers with Mars and Venus. Are we chiefly to
remember Homer, in whose *Odyssey* the two Olympians,
trapped in an adulterous affair and exposed in the absurdity of
love's postures in a net they cannot break, move our superior
laughter—as do, in one of their dimensions, Antony and
Cleopatra? Are we to remember, too, the Renaissance taste for
paintings and engravings that show a Mars vanquished by
Venus, victim or trophy of love's power, her *amorini* sporting
with his armor, and he himself languid or asleep, or, in some
instances, chained and fettered to her throne? And is it per-
tinent to recall further that the intention of these images often
turns out to be more complex than at first glance we might
suppose? For the two deities are, in some instances, to be
understood as emblems of contrary qualities, male force and
female grace, now in a work of art ideally reconciled; and
even, in others, as the contrary powers of Strife and Love,
which tie the universe together and from whose union, according to Plutarch, the goddess Harmony is born.[4]

Antony, like Mars in the paintings, grows conscious of
love's "fetters";[5] loses or is threatened with the loss of man-
hood, as the fanning eunuchs in I, i warn us; and at long last
acknowledges himself (as he was also obliged to do the day she
came down the Cydnus) Cleopatra's captive in a "Triumph of
Love." But the crucial question that remains—in the play as in
the painted figures of Mars and Venus—is what the triumph
means. I believe that Shakespeare throws some light on the

4. Edgar Wind, *Pagan Mysteries in the Renaissance* (Harmondsworth, Middlesex: Penguin Books, Ltd., 1967), pp. 85-86.
5. Love's fetters are vividly allegorized in the chains that bind
Spenser's Amoret to the brazen pillar in the House of Busyrane (*Faerie
Queene*, III, xii, 30, 37, 41).

perplexities of this question in the scene that reunites the
lovers after the middle day of Actium, when for the time being
Antony and his men have had the victory (IV, viii). As he
enters, still clad in full armor, he thanks his soldiers with characteristic élan and generosity. Then he sees Cleopatra, stops (as
I read the scene) in his tracks bedazzled (leaving us in the
audience to imagine his emotions as he finds himself once
more in his old role of redoubtable captain returning to a
radiant queen), and then, with an intensity of adoration that
ignores all onlookers, bursts forth in one of the most winning
speeches of the play:

> O thou day o' th' world,
> Chain mine armed neck, leap thou, attire and all,
> Through proof of harness to my heart, and there
> Ride on the pants triumphing.

(IV, viii, 13-16)

The image of Cleopatra riding the great beats of Antony's
heart (a heart that, as we know from earlier comment, "in the
scuffles of great fights hath burst The buckles on his breast")
as if it were a high-mettled steed on which she is carried in a
triumph that he—her prisoner, "chained"—adorns, is breath-
taking and becomes more so when we reflect on what we see:
for though in the language she is conqueror and he her captive,
in the scene he is conqueror too and has indeed freely bestowed this conquest on her, as his victorious presence, in full
armor, attests. The episode forces upon our consciousness a
recognition of the very different kind of triumph that they
have within their power as lovers from the kind for which
Caesar seeks him, and the two competing value systems, theirs
and Caesar's, hang for a brief instant in the eye as well as in
the ear, as she runs to be embraced. Then, leaning back and
devouring him with her gaze, she kindles sublimely to the
occasion, catching his image in an answering image of her own:

> Lord of lords!
> O infinite virtue, com'st thou smiling from
> The world's great snare uncaught?

(IV, viii, 16-18)

Does she, by her "world's great snare," mean the wars? Does
she, on the contrary, mean Caesar, who is soon to become
"universal landlord" and "sole sir o' the world"? Or does she

simply mean, as a recent editor phrases it, "all the snares the world can set," understanding by "world" everything, inner as well as outer, that the play accumulates to threaten love? No matter. As with Roman triumphs versus Antony's "triumphing," we are obviously to let this "snare" reverberate against another order of captivity altogether, an order implicit at this moment in Antony's "chain my armed neck," explicit earlier in his "These strong Egyptian fetters I must break," and evoked again, tellingly, at the play's end, when, as we saw, Caesar speaks of "her strong toil of grace." There, once again, the two attitudes will hang against each other in the mind and invite us to consider that there are more kinds of captivity and of triumph than any Caesar dreams of.

VI

The other sorts of evocation that Shakespeare sets in motion in *Antony and Cleopatra* derive from the themes and conventions of Renaissance love poetry, notably the sonnet. Individualizing and psychological, these strongly counter the play's tendencies toward moral exemplum and allegory, establishing it still more intransigently in the domain of paradox, where contradiction thrives. Though the ultimate effect of this body of evocation is to bring before the mind of the spectator a unified and highly plausible experience of passion, we may nevertheless separate out for our present purpose two divergent strains, answering to the *amo* and *odi* of the Latin love poets, the *amare* and *amaro* of the Italian. The *odi-amare* strain in *Antony and Cleopatra* is best grasped by comparison and contrast with Shakespeare's treatment of it in his sonnets to and about the Dark Lady. In both cases, we have an affair between experienced lovers, "orbited nice" (to borrow a phrase of John Crowe Ransom's), in an intense relationship that contains comedy and tragedy, and, to the man at least, brings disgust and pain as often as love and pleasure. In both we find a mistress very like a parody of the delicate blonde *belle dame sans merci* of the sonneteering convention, who is always indescribably remote and chaste; a woman who in the sonnets is notably blackhaired as well as hearted, and in the play, whatever we may decide about her heart, has a tawny

skin ("with Phoebus' amorous pinches black," I, v, 28), and a
voluptuous disposition. Both mistresses have a remarkable—in
the sonnets it is also sinister—power to make ill things look
attractive. "For vilest things," says Enobarbus, at the end of
his famous account of Cleopatra, so

> Become themselves in her, that the holy priests
> *(II, ii, 239-41)* Bless her when she is riggish.

The poet of the sonnets confronts the same puzzle:

> Whence hast thou this becoming of things ill,
> That in the very refuse of thy deeds
> There is such strength and warrantise of skill
> That in my mind thy worst all best exceeds?
> Who taught thee how to make me love thee more,
> *(Sonnet 150)* The more I hear and see just cause to hate?

These are lines that a lesser Antony, trimmed and barbered to
the sonnet's narrow room, might have uttered after watching
Cleopatra put out her hand for Thidias to kiss.

Such "treason" is precisely a further resemblance between
the sonnets' story and the play's. Both mistresses, in one sense
or other, are capable of playing their lovers false; have, or have
had, other men; and though Cleopatra is not, so far as we are
ever reliably told, unfaithful to Antony within the time of the
play, she uses locutions in referring to her former affair with
Pompey's father that may suggest a conscious or unconscious
link tying her to the treacherous dark lady in the poet's mind.
For as she waits for Antony to return from Rome—feeding
herself "With most delicious poison," as she puts it—she muses
how when Julius Caesar was alive, she was already "A morsel
for a monarch," and how "great Pompey"

> Would stand and make his eyes grow in my brow;
> There would he anchor his aspect, and die
> *(I, v, 31-34)* With looking on his life.

The individual words in these lines are alive with erotic possibilities; just how alive one can best see by placing them beside
the appropriate verses of Sonnet 137, where likewise a woman
is the sea, and men are the ships that anchor there:

If eyes, corrupt by over-partial looks,
Be anchored in the bay where all men ride,
Why of eyes' falsehood hast thou forgèd hooks
Whereto the judgment of my heart is tied?
Why should my heart think that a several plot
Which my heart knows the wide world's common place?
Or mine eyes seeing this, say this is not,
To put fair truth upon so foul a face?

Allowing again for the difference between dramatic speech and
lyric, this could be Antony speaking after Thidias has been
taken to be whipped, for it is certainly his theme:

You have been a boggler ever:
But when we in our viciousness grow hard
(O misery on't!) the wise gods seel our eyes,
In our own filth drop our clear judgments; make us
Adore our errors, laugh at 's while we strut
To our confusion.

(III, xiii, 110-15)

To conclude, both affairs "puddle"—this is Desdemona's word
for the effect of Othello's jealousy—the clear spirit of the
lover. Both describe what, at one level of the experience, or at
least when viewed in one way (in *Antony and Cleopatra*, usually the Roman way), is unqualified lust: "Th' expense of spirit
in a waste of shame" (Sonnet 129). And both eventuate in a
perpetual unrest which rises to peaks of anguish and self-loath-
ing akin to madness. Antony feels that he has been poisoned
with the shirt of Nessus, and in his last towering rage Cleopatra
takes him to have run mad:

more mad
Than Telamon for his shield; the boar of Thessaly
Was never so embossed.

(IV, xiii, 1-3)

The speaker of the sonnets sees his condition in like terms. It
is an incurable disease which brings on madness and must end
in death because his reason, like Antony's Enobarbus in the
play, has given him up for lost. When seen against Antony's
continuous fluctuations from disgust to reconciliation, and
against the movements of Enobarbus, who acts as reason's
spokesman in the play, the whole of Sonnet 147 becomes
luminous:

My love is as a fever, longing still
For that which longer nurseth the disease,
Feeding on that which doth preserve the ill,
Th' uncertain sickly appetite to please.
My reason, the physician to my love,
Angry that his prescriptions are not kept,
Hath left me, and I desperate now approve
Desire is death, which physic did except.
Past cure I am, now reason is past care,
And frantic-mad with evermore unrest;
My thoughts and my discourse as madmen's are,
At random from the truth vainly expressed:
    For I have sworn thee fair, and thought thee bright,
    Who art as black as hell, as dark as night.

Such likenesses are seductive; but they are also extremely unspecific, and it would be folly to argue from them that the love affair in the play in any precise way reflects that in the sonnet sequence. The tone of the sonnet love affair is, in any case, far more acrid, cynical, corrosive. The play's lovers are repeatedly caught up into regions of feeling, and touch on images and idioms of romantic amplification and adulation, that the lover who speaks in the Dark Lady sonnets avoids, or uses only to belittle; and the literary territory on which Shakespeare levies for this affirmative side of his *odi et amo* polarity is visibly a system of Petrarchan attitudes and conventions whose general emphasis on immutability and steadfastness creates an interesting antithesis to our sense of a world in flux.

We should remark in this connection, first of all, the exuberant vein of compliment that Antony so often has recourse to, tributes of the perfect lover to his dazzling lady. Cleopatra's eye, he tells us, "becked forth" his wars "and called them home" (IV, xii, 26). Her bosom was his "crownet," his "chief end" (l. 27). "Eternity" was in her lips and eyes, "Bliss" in her brows' bent (I, iii, 35-36). Her hand, even in one of his great rages, remains for him "this kingly seal, And plighter of high hearts" (III, xiii, 125-26). Her beauty and vitality, like those of every sonneteer's mistress, make her equal to the sun ("O thou day o' th' world" [IV, viii, 13]) and to the moon ("our terrene moon Is now eclips'd" [III, xiii,

153-54]). Her tears outvalue empires ("Fall not a tear, I say: one of them rates All that is won and lost" [III, xi, 69-70]), and when she dies, brightness falls from the air ("since the torch is out, Lie down, and stray no farther" [IV, xiv, 46-47]). All these praises Cleopatra reciprocates with an abandon that is new to the tradition only because the speaker is a woman: Antony is her "man of men" (I, v, 72), her "Lord of lords" (IV, viii, 16), "infinite virtue" (l. 17), "the crown o' th' earth" (IV, xv, 63), "our jewel" (l. 81), and "nature's piece 'gainst fancy" (V, ii, 99), that is to say, nature's masterpiece surpassing anything the imagination can create. For her, too, attraction continues even when she is most repelled: "Though he be painted one way like a Gorgon, The other way's a Mars" (II, v, 116-17); and for her, too, light goes out of the world with his death: "Ah, women, women, look! Our lamp is spent, it's out! " (IV, xv, 87-88); indeed, all light should go out—

> O sun,
> Burn the great sphere thou mov'st in, darkling stand
> The varying shore o' th' world!   *(IV, xv, 9-11)*

—for there is nothing left to see on earth that is remarkable, even for "the visiting moon" (l. 68).

Further to be noticed are the frequent individual usages of this tradition that the play calls in. Some are instantly recognizable despite the new force that a dramatic context usually brings them. One thinks here particularly of the reworking of the commonplace comparison of love's sighs and tears to winds and floods[6] that takes place in Enobarbus's comment on Cleopatra's emotional resources—

We cannot call her winds and waters sighs and tears: they are greater storms and tempests than almanacs can report. This cannot be cunning in her; if it be, she makes a shower of rain as well as Jove;   *(I, ii, 145-48)*

—or of the handsome version of the absent-yet-present formula contained in Antony's final words to her as he leaves for Rome—

6. Spenser allegorizes these in the thunder, lightning, earthquake, and "hideous storme of winde" surrounding the House of Busyrane *(Faerie Queene,* III, xii, 2).

Our separation so abides and flies
That thou residing here goes yet with me,
(I, iii, 102-4) And I hence fleeting here remain with thee;

—or of the entombment of the beloved's name in the lover's breast, adapted by Mardian to give verisimilitude to his baroque tale of Cleopatra's death (and by Shakespeare, I suspect, to give a possibly sexual and certainly comic edge to the whole proceeding):

                    The last she spake
Was "Antony! most noble Antony!"
Then in the midst a tearing groan did break
The name of Antony; it was divided
(IV, xiv, 29- Between her heart and lips: she rendered life,
34) Thy name so buried in her.

Other formulas from the sonneteers' thesaurus have been so thoroughly reworked in the playwright's imagination that their identity is difficult to be sure of. The idea, for example, that love's bondage is the highest freedom ("To enter in these bonds, is to be free," says Donne),[7] which presumably survives among the meanings intended by Shakespeare, though not by Caesar, in the reference to Cleopatra's "strong toil of grace," and which is almost certainly implicit in the great reunion of the lovers already noticed: "Chain mine armed neck," "com'st thou smiling from The world's great snare uncaught?" Or the idea of the lover's dream of his beloved, which brings her so vividly before his senses that he wakes longing for its return, and even questioning the reality of what he wakes to as compared with his dream-vision. This experience is given in the play to the beloved after her lover's death ("O such another sleep, that I might see But such another man!"), and the weighing of the two realities of dream and wake, the latter intensified by Dolabella's skepticism, is handled with a virtuosity that teases us out of thought:

7. Donne, *Elegie XIX: To His Mistris Going to Bed.* In *To Althea, from Prison,* Lovelace has:

When I lie tangled in her hair,
And fettered to her eye,
The gods that wanton in the air
Know no such liberty.

Cleopatra: Think you there was or might be such a man
  As this I dreamt of?
Dolabella: Gentle madam, no.
Cleopatra: You lie, up to the hearing of the gods.
  But if there be nor ever were one such,
  It's past the size of dreaming: nature wants stuff
  To vie strange forms with fancy, yet t' imagine
  An Antony were nature's piece 'gainst fancy,
  Condemning shadows quite.   *(V, ii, 93-100)*

Or again, the idea that, after creating the beloved, Nature
broke the mold, so that now she remains the sole model on
earth of ideal beauty and virtue, together with the corollary
that, in making her, Nature produced an excellence unmatchable by Art. Chaucer has some attractive lines on this in *The
Physician's Tale:*

Fair was this mayde in excellent beautee
Aboven every wight that man may see;
For Nature hath with sovereyn diligencë
Y-formed hir in so greet excellencë
As though she wolde seyn, 'lo! I, Naturë,
Thus can I forme and peynte a creaturë,
Whan that me list; who can me countrefetë?
Pigmalion noght, though he ay forge and betë,
Or grave, or peyntë; for I dar wel seyn,
Apelles, Zanzis, sholdë werche in veyn,
Outher to grave or peynte or forge or betë,
If they presumèd me to countrefetë."   *(7-18)*

Shakespeare returns to the theme twice, once in the passage
just quoted from Cleopatra's dream of Antony and once in
Enobarbus's description of Cleopatra:

    For her own person,
It beggared all description: she did lie
In her pavilion, cloth-of-gold of tissue
O'erpicturing that Venus where we see   *(II, ii, 198-*
The fancy outwork nature.   *202)*

and it would not be hard to believe that in one or both of
these Chaucer was in his mind. Or yet again: the conventional
idea of the beloved's heavenly face as object of the lover's only

true astronomy.[8] This too, in the play, is given to the beloved
and amplified to a magnitude consonant with the play's general hyperbolic style:

His face was as the heav'ns, and therein stuck
A sun and moon, which kept their course, and lighted
(V, ii, 79-81) The little O, th' earth.

For a final instance, thoroughly problematic, we may consider the idea of the lover as a bark or vessel which is ship-
wrecked by the storms of passion and the cruelties of his lady,
an idea that may or may not linger somewhere in the dim
background of Enobarbus's aside:

                                      Sir, sir, thou art so leaky
(III, xiii, 63- That we must leave thee to thy sinking, for
65) Thy dearest quit thee.

VII

Easily the two most important derivatives in *Antony and
Cleopatra* from the formulas of love poetry are the idea of
love-as-space, and the closely related idea of love-as-war already touched on in connection with the figures of Mars and
Venus. These, I believe, are the presiding structural ideas of
the play, and their presence is felt at every point. Love-as-war
may be glanced at briefly because its influence is transparent.
All the conventions of the sonneteers and courtly love poets
on this theme—Sidney's "dear captainness," Petrarch's "O
dolce mia guerriera," the common notion of the beloved as
"dearest enemy," the metaphors of love's encounters, duels,
sieges, arrows, armor, the puns on killing, dying, and being
slain, still vigorous as late as Pope's time—all these unverbalize
themselves in *Antony and Cleopatra* to become explicitly or
implicitly exemplified in the dramatic action. The lady's arm-
ing her knight for combat appears in the play in the form of an
actual aubade scene (IV, iv), where Venus-Cleopatra fumbles
tenderly with Mars-Antony's armor. The "warrior-lady" appears in the form of a warrior-lady who goes to the wars in

8. Sidney's *Arcadia* in *Works*, ed. Albert Feuillerat (Cambridge:
Cambridge University Press, 1922-26), 1:375, has some interesting
turns on this. Shakespeare's use of the convention in *Antony and Cleopatra* may owe something to Marlowe's *Tamburlaine*, II, i, 467 ff.

fact: "And as the president of my kingdom will Appear there for a man" (III, vii, 17-18). The "death-wound" given the sonnet-lover by his mistress's eyes, as in Sidney's twentieth ("Fly, fly, my friends, I have my death wound; fly!") substantiates in the play into a real death wound, for which the mistress is responsible even if she does not give it, and into a situation whose likeness to the one imagined in Sidney is signaled by Decretas's cry: "Thy death and fortunes bid thy followers fly." Similarly, the lyric lover's ingenious play on "love" and "honor"—

True, a new mistress now I chase,
The first foe in the field;
And with a stronger faith embrace
A sword, a horse, a shield.

Yet this inconstancy is such
As you too shall adore;
I could not love thee, dear, so much,
Loved I not honor more

—finds at Shakespeare's hands a massive development in terms of Antony's predicament throughout the play; and likewise the lyric lover's semantic game with supposedly alternative kinds of warfare—

Till I have peace with thee, warr other Men,
And when I have peace, can I leave thee then?
. . . .
Here lett me warr; in these arms lett me lye;
Here lett me parlee, batter, bleede, and dye

—enlarges into whole scenes of anguish as, in the play, the two wars prove to be inseparable and love's war the more ruinous of the two.

For in Antony, passion is not the isolable experience that it is in Donne and Lovelace.[9] It is a part of all he is, and therefore part and parcel of his soldiership, in which it finds expression, and which finds expression in it. Warring cannot be isolated from loving:

9. Donne, *Elegie XX: Love's Warre*, and Lovelace, *To Lucasta, Going to the Wars*.

I made these wars for Egypt, and the Queen,
Whose heart I thought I had, for she had mine.

Nor can loving be isolated from warring, from the political and
military ascendancy that a million loyal supporters guarantee:

Whose heart I thought I had, for she had mine,
Which, whilst it was mine, had annexed unto 't
A million moe, now lost.

Decay of love is tied irrevocably to decay of imperial glory:

she, Eros, has

*(IV, xiv, 15
ff.)*
Packed cards with Caesar, and false-played my glory
Unto an enemy's triumph;

and conversely, his Roman enemy's "triumph" (used here with
a pun on "trump"), if it has been assisted by Cleopatra, pre-
cludes forever the kind of triumph in which his "dearest enemy" once rode "on the pants triumphing."

The other presiding idea, love-as-space (space that is to be
discovered, explored, claimed, possessed), is of course intimately allied to love-as-war, but serves, I think, a subtler function, opening immediately into the play's geographical magni-
tudes. For the lover, throughout the tradition we are considering, love constitutes an "empire"; and the beloved (from love's
infinitely expansionist and sometimes erotically exploratory
point of view) is considered spatially in various ways: as coun-
tryside, garden, orchard, park, tillage ("I'll be thy park, and
thou shalt be my deer";[10] "She made great Caesar lay his
sword to bed; He ploughed her, and she cropped" [II, ii,
227-28]); or as a rich new land for voyages of discovery and
commerce—spice island, continent, or hemisphere:

O my America! my new-found-land,
My kingdome safeliest when with one man man'd,
My Myne of precious stones, My Emperie,
How blest am I in this discovering thee! [11]

or best of all as a world:

For love, all love of other sights controules,

10. Shakespeare, *Venus and Adonis*, l. 231.
11. Donne, *Elegie XIX: To His Mistris Going to Bed*.

And makes one little roome, an every where.
Let sea-discoverers to new worlds have gone,
Let Maps to other, worlds on worlds have showne,
Let us possesse one world, each hath one, and is one.[12]

What Shakespeare does in the play is to give this literary formula—together with the psychological and emotional "truth" it incorporates, the heart's systolic and diastolic fervor now amplifying the person of the beloved to include in her person all being and all meaning, now contracting all being and meaning so that they may be contained in her person—a reinterpretation in dramatic terms. The play's political and geographical grandeurs, its struggles of great personages for "empire," enable him to create, in a subtle psychological sense to which Kenneth Burke has shrewdly called attention,[13] an objective correlative, or "ostentation," of the expansionist phase of passion, with its rapturous self-assertions, shows of power, and displaced gestures of aggression. In this light may be seen Antony's greeting to Cleopatra through Alexas:

Say the firm Roman to great Egypt sends
This treasure of an oyster; at whose foot,
To mend the petty present, I will piece
Her opulent throne with kingdoms. All the east
(Say thou) shall call her mistress.   *(I, v, 43-47)*

Both lovers write large, in the marketplace of Alexandria and on the maps of Asia, the erotic energies of their union, as Caesar's description of the occasion seems to understand:

Caesar: Contemning Rome, he has done all this and more
     In Alexandria. Here's the manner of 't:
     I' th' market-place on a tribunal silvered,
     Cleopatra and himself in chairs of gold
     Were publicly enthroned; at the feet sat
     Caesarion, whom they call my father's son,
     And all the unlawful issue that their lust
     Since then hath made between them. Unto her
     He gave the stablishment of Egypt; made her

12. Donne, *The Good-Morrow*, ll. 10-14.
13. *Language as Symbolic Action* (Berkeley: University of California Press, 1966), p. 101.

> Of lower Syria, Cyprus, Lydia,
> Absolute queen.
> *Maecenas:* This in the public eye?
> *Caesar:* I' th' common show-place, where they exercise.
> His sons he there proclaimed the kings of kings:
> Great Media, Parthia, and Armenia
> He gave to Alexander; to Ptolemy he assigned
> Syria, Cilicia, and Phoenicia. She
> In the habiliments of the goddess Isis
> That day appeared, and oft before gave audience,
> *(III, vi, 1-19)*   As 'tis reported, so.

With the same tumescent overtones, at the close, Cleopatra cherishes her dream of an Antony who is emotionally and spatially realized simultaneously, a sort of psycho-cosmos whose arm crests the world and whose voice is propertied as all the tuned spheres.

The contrary or contractive impulses of passion find *their* correlative, one supposes, in Cleopatra's monument and the long decrescendo that brings Antony to it. There, whatever it may signify, the lovers are reunited for the last time in the play; Antony dies in Cleopatra's arms (the only "space" now left him); and she also dies, robed and crowned, on a throne that is in fact a bed. "Every where"—to read the reverse face of Donne's coin—has now become "one little roome." The paths of glory have led (like all paths) to a grave. And love has been dissolved in death, except that dying has proved to be a manifestation of love, in more senses than one. To go beyond this is to risk saying far too much, though additional ghostly figures from Petrarchan and other repertories—of the beloved as a fortress under siege by death and time; of Desire as an infant at the breast of nurse Beauty; of the worm (serpent and what more?) as death's but also love's and immortality's agent, as the clown's malapropisms seem to hint; and of another kind of "monument," more durable than brass and loftier than the pyramids—may well continue to float troublingly, for some, about the final scenes.

VIII

Antony's death is followed by a moment when Cleopatra

faints and lies as still as he:

Charmian: O quietness, lady!
Iras: She's dead too, our sovereign.   *(IV, xv, 69-70)*

Then her women succeed in rousing her, she speaks her resolve
to do as he has done, and they go out together, *"bearing off
Antony's body."* Cleopatra's death is followed by a similar
moment, more prolonged. After she is dead, Charmian
straightens her crown, speaks proudly to Caesar's guard (who
has rushed in to check on his prisoners) of what has been
done—what has been "well done, and fitting for a princess
Descended of so many royal kings"—then falls herself. There is
an entry by Dolabella, and a full ceremonial entry by *"Caesar
and all his Train, marching."* They theorize about the deaths,
Caesar renders his epitaph, which receives the lovers into
"story," and announces a solemn funeral, after which, "to
Rome." They go out—again marching, one presumes—carrying
Cleopatra's bed, her motionless figure sitting or half-reclining
on it, robed and crowned.

The sensory effect of both these moments is very powerful.
Basically, in stage terms, it comes from the difference between
absolute stillness and purposeful movement. In the movers, life
goes on, as we know it must; their history will be fulfilled. In
the immobile, history has already been fulfilled; it has departed from them, and something else has replaced it. But what? Is
it a dignity, such as perhaps we always attribute to those who
have drunk the whole of experience, the ultimate stillness as
well as the movement that leads there? Is it an exultation that
they are, as Shakespeare says elsewhere, "past the tyrant's
stroke," past the whips and scorns of time? Is it a serenity got
from the same source as poets when they are laid asleep in
body to become a living soul, seeing into the life of things? Or
is it simply that absolute stillness has some sort of indefinable
absolute claim on the human imagination, being the thing
most opposite to what we know at first hand in the diurnal
world, where, as in this play, everything slips and slides and
rots itself with motion?

Whatever the explanation, I never read or see these two
scenes acted without concluding that the unresolved polarities
they contain—life against death, movement against stillness,

change against something that has shackled accidents and
bolted up change, history against something that is no longer
temporal—has something to say to us about Shakespeare's pro-
cedure in the play as a whole with its long series of similarly
unresolved oppositions: Egypt and Rome, politics and love,
public life and private, loyalty and self-interest, grandeur and
humility, mobility and constancy, and many more pairs that
one may accumulate by reading the critics. For the play seems
founded, in my own experience of it—not founded accidental-
ly, but creatively, painstakingly—on the same sort of defiant
pluralism that we find in other deeply paradoxical works, such
as *The Praise of Folly* or *Don Quixote*. As in Erasmus, we have
in the play one perspective which knows that Folly is always
folly, a consuming and illicit passion always ruinous, and another perspective which sees that some follies may be less
foolish than the world's cherished wisdom, an imperium in the
embrace of Cleopatra more life-giving than an imperium in
Rome. Neither perspective cancels the other out, both are
"true." In Cervantes, the representative of an imagined literary world of perfect chivalry is set down in seventeenth-century Spain, suffers bravely and comically the incongruities that
result, refuses to be discomfited, and at last persuades us that
his vision of things has a valency of its own. Something of this
sort happens also in our play. Antony, ever attracted by the
sweeping magnanimity of his nature to an imagined literary
world of perfect devotion between man and woman (as the
first line he speaks to us shows: "There's beggary in the love
that can be reckon'd"), is set down in the slippery Roman
world he has himself helped create, suffers deeply—but always
too, like Quixote, a little comically—from the incongruities
between the code he is attracted to and that world's demands,
yet refuses equally to be discomfited (either by Cleopatra's
treasons or his own), and in the end wagers with his life that
there is a valency in the code's perspective, though again it can
never cancel out the world's perspective, since both are true.

Shakespeare's play is not a *Praise of Folly*, despite certain
affinities that were mentioned at the beginning of this essay.
Still less is it a *Don Quixote de la Mancha*. It has its own
metabolism. Yet I think the thrust of history in it, the pres-
sures of mobility and mutability which lead inexorably to An-

tony's ruin and Caesar's triumph, are countered, to a degree, by the traditions of ideal devotion, and of escape from mutability through love, that are implied in the Petrarchan and romance idiom in which both lovers have been immersed by their creator. Plainly, the world of history is unfriendly to these principles, as it is unfriendly also to Quixote's chivalric fiction, and in the end they are likely to be compromised or betrayed, as happens repeatedly in the play. Yet they speak for something that is durable in the human heart, something no more but also no less true to our experience than the nightmare of history from which, like Stephen Dedalus, we all struggle in our several fashions to escape; and I believe that Shakespeare saw this, as he moved in the romances that follow *Antony and Cleopatra* toward defining an alternative: an alternative that has never failed in its power to move the imagination, whether we think, like Dante, of the love that moves the sun and other stars; or, like Spenser, of the time to come when "all shall changèd bee, And from thenceforth none no more change shall see"; or, like Keats, of the bright star whose steadfastness he longs to reconcile with his living breathing passion for Fanny Brawne; or, most recently, like T. S. Eliot, of the still center without which there would be no turning wheel:

> Except for the point, the still point,
> There would be no dance, and there is only the dance.

Shakespeare's Careless Art
T. J. B. SPENCER

5

Shakespeare critics generally show a bias toward his mind or toward his art. There are critics who take for granted his art and concentrate their attention (in a variety of ways) upon his moral sensibility. And there are critics who are fascinated by Shakespeare's art, and take for granted the moral refinement that can be extracted from his plays, or are sometimes even skeptical of its existence.

I propose to state and explore one or two of the problems of judging Shakespeare's art. Only incidentally do I comment upon his mind and morality. Not that I would wish to appear to disparage Shakespeare's mind and morality. On the contrary, I feel confident that Shakespeare's mind was the most cunning, and his morality the most enigmatic or enlightened, of any author I have read. But one small aspect of Shakespeare is usually enough to consider at a time. The magnitude of the author and the weight of his critical bibliography are such that writers on Shakespeare must, by their very choice of such a subject, be brave men, or at least rash men; when possible they should set themselves narrow bounds.

In considering the nature of Shakespeare's art, it is reasonable to begin the inquiry with the question, what did Shakespeare think of his own writings? He failed to provide us with his literary memoirs. For him we lack anything like Ben Jonson's literary notebooks, or that ironical poem of Lope de Vega on the art of writing stage plays (*Arte nuevo de hacer comedias en este tiempo*), or the *Dichtung und Wahrheit* of Goethe, or *The Prelude*, or Keats's letters. Shakespeare's most lengthy and serious piece of criticism concerns not the art of poetry or the art of drama, but the art of acting. As a full-time professional man of the theater, he was perhaps most deeply concerned with the techniques of his own profession; and the famous passage in *Hamlet* is memorable not only for its content or meaning but also for its sophistication of language.

Perhaps also, like many actors and dramatists, he was not favorable to literary critics. He does not go so far as the author of *Waiting for Godot*, by whom the word "critic" is used as the climax of a series of invectives. In Shakespeare's plays there are plenty of jokes about poets and poetry, about nature and art and inspiration, about the genres and the figures of speech. Perhaps most interesting of all is that Poet in *Timon of Athens*, a cunningly drawn figure; a combination of false modesty, self-centeredness, and verbal flow; an unflattering picture of the professional men of letters whom Shakespeare must sometimes have met—not the theater men like Shakespeare himself, but the professionals who stood up for the dignity of literature; perhaps that rival poet with "the proud full sail of his great verse"; he who drew inspiration from

> that affable familiar ghost
> *(Sonnet 86)* Which nightly gulls him with intelligence.

—all those who wrote to be read, and who disparaged stage plays even though they sometimes condescended to employ their pens on them. There was Samuel Daniel and the circle of the Countess of Pembroke; Ben Jonson in some of his moods; John Webster, who lacked an "understanding auditory"; writers of tragedies, perhaps, rather than comedies; those who doubtless felt as Marston explained in the address "To My Equal Reader" before *Parasitaster, or The Fawne* in 1606:

Comedies are writ to be spoken, not read: Remember the life of these things consists in action; and for your such courteous survay of my pen, I will present a Tragedy to you which shall boldly abide the most curious perusall.

Marston's words are surely remarkable. Were Shakespeare's plays, or at least his tragedies, written to "abide the most curious perusall"? Are they works of art that can legitimately be the subject of "the most curious perusall"? This notion of "most curious perusall" is what is, after all, characteristic of modern Shakespeare criticism. And it has an interesting histo-

ry. The eighteenth-century critics of Shakespeare busied themselves in cataloguing Shakespeare's beauties and faults. It was a
sensitive kind of practical criticism. The critics found many
beauties; but they were not so much overwhelmed by the
beauties as not to comment manfully on Shakespeare's faults.
Some of the faultfinding was absurd. But, good or bad, it was
all preserved in the Variorum editions of Shakespeare up to
1821 and remained a constant provocation and irritation to
critics of the next generation. For the nineteenth century had,
on the whole, a new principle of Shakespeare criticism.
Shakespeare's Julius Caesar, in a canceled line of the play,
asserted that he did never wrong but with just cause. Shakespeare, too, it was discovered, never did artistic wrong but with
just cause. One of the tasks of criticism became that of demonstrating that the supposed faults were in fact beauties. It
became one of the palmary achievements of a critic to demonstrate that one of Shakespeare's blunders was in fact a superb
stroke of Shakespearean artistry: that, for example, the
drunken porter's scene in *Macbeth* was highly relevant to the
play; and that both the mouse and the rat in Shakespeare's
most famous tragedy were not in ghastly bad taste, but exquisitely appropriate.

This attitude to Shakespeare has become widespread; and
both the professional critics and those amateur critics who
produce Shakespeare's plays in our professional theaters find it
hard to resist the temptation to prove that some bit of apparent difficulty or absurdity or irrelevance is highly con-
gruous with the structure or thematic development of the
play, or at least "works on the stage." Shakespeare, wrote
Emerson on our behalf, displays "a merit so incessant, that
each reader is incredulous of the perception of other readers"
(*Representative Men*). For some of us all the time, and for
most of us some of the time, he habitually lifts the human
mind into regions where questions of artistic fallibility and
technical scrupulosity become irrelevant.

It is unlikely, however, that Shakespeare solved all his artistic problems with equally consummate artistry. It is also unlikely that we always understand his art. We confidently assert
that some plays are better than others. Hazlitt and Henry
Irving thought that *Love's Labour's Lost* was the worst of

Shakespeare's plays. G. Wilson Knight seems to think that *Timon of Athens* is his best. Most of us disagree with these opinions.

The artistry of the beginnings of Shakespeare's plays has been much praised. Some plays begin with a striking or noisy episode, attracting or demanding attention (*Hamlet, Macbeth*). Some begin with a quiet conversation, which shows a certain confidence in gaining the attention of the audience. This is true both of tragedy (*Othello, King Lear*) and of comedy *(The Merchant of Venice, Much Ado About Nothing, As You Like It)*.

The artistry of the endings of the plays has not received such widespread approval. Nor is it so easy to defend or explicate. I take a well-known example. In Lodge's *Rosalynde*, as we expect in a work of prose narrative, there are episodes that are drastically compressed in the later part of *As You Like It*. In *Rosalynde*, Fernandyne, the second son of Sir John of Bordeaux, "that lives a scholar in Paris," brings the news to the exiles in the Forest of Arden that the twelve peers of France have risen against the usurping monarch Torismond. Thereupon, Gerismond, the rightful but banished king, joins the peers, along with Saladyne and Rosader. Torismond is defeated and killed in a bloody battle; and the story ends with the settlement of the kingdom.

Shakespeare clearly has no time for this sort of thing, for he needs to wind up the plot of his play. Quite disgracefully, he brings the "Second Brother" on to the stage to announce the news: the usurping Duke has been converted, and so the rightful Duke can reassume his dignity without a blow being struck.

> Duke Frederick, hearing how that every day
> Men of great worth resorted to this forest,
> Addressed a mighty power, which were on foot,
> In his own conduct, purposely to take
> His brother here and put him to the sword;
> And to the skirts of this wild wood he came,
> Where, meeting with an old religious man,
> After some question with him, was converted
> Both from his enterprise and from the world;
> His crown bequeathing to his banished brother,

And all their lands restored to them again
That were with him exiled.[1]　　　　　　　　　　　　*(V, iv, 160-71)*

Dr. Johnson objected to this rapid trick to give the play a comfortable conclusion: "By hastening to the end of his work, Shakespeare suppressed the dialogue between the usurper and the hermit, and lost an opportunity of exhibiting a moral lesson in which he might have found matter worthy of his highest powers."[2] Both the title and the treatment of *As You Like It* discourage us from taking the situation as seriously as that. Yet the last scenes in some of Shakespeare's greatest comedies have been the subject of acerb censure and eager defense. No one complains of a few speedy deaths to wind up a tragedy or a tragical history. But any instant happiness to wind up a comedy is often felt by Shakespeare's more earnest admirers to be offensive.

The endings of plays are not to be analyzed too closely on psychological or ideological grounds. After two or more hours' traffic on the stage, the audience is tired and is beginning to feel it wants to go home. The perceptions are relaxed. An economical dramatist does not put too much into that last ten minutes. Wisely he concentrates his efforts on giving a general impression of satisfaction; in comedy, certainly; and generally, too, in its own way, in tragedy. The censures and defenses of some of the last scenes of Shakespeare's greatest comedies mistake his artistry. In *Measure for Measure*, for example, Angelo certainly gets off lightly. Some critics have become enraged by his being spared so easily. Even admirers like Swinburne felt that occasionally Shakespeare lapsed from high artistic seriousness and made concessions or sacrifices to theatrical taste that were contrary to his own moral judgments. *Measure for Measure*, he thought, cries out for a tragic ending:

The actual or hypothetical necessity of pairing off all the couples after such a fashion as to secure a nominally happy and undeniably matrimonial ending is the theatrical idol whose

---

1. The text of Shakespeare's plays is that of the New Penguin Shakespeare. The line-numbering is that of the Globe edition.
2. Samuel Johnson, *Dr. Johnson on Shakespeare*, ed. W. K. Wimsatt (Harmondsworth and Baltimore: Penguin Shakespeare Library, 1969), p. 107.

tyranny exacts this holocaust of higher and better feelings than the mere liquorish desire to leave the board of fancy with a palatable morsel of cheap sugar on the tongue.[3]

Certainly Angelo's repentance is brief. He is given no opportunity to explain himself. The wrongs he has committed have a baseness and malevolence about them, and they ought to be expiated. But while (in cold blood) we agree with this, do we really, during the last few minutes of the play, want to hear Angelo explaining his state of mind at length, demonstrating that he really does deserve his virtuous Mariana after all, or volunteering to spend a year in a hospital among the sick and dying in order to convince the world of his change of heart? Not at that point in the play. Shakespeare's "moral indifference" is merely the discretion of an intelligently economical dramatist, one who does not waste his precious artistic energy, abundant though it may have been, when there is no need for it.

Other villains besides Angelo in Shakespeare's comedies can be judged to get off lightly. In *The Tempest* Antonio and Sebastian have plotted the murder of their King, and have only been thwarted in their cruel, ambitious plot by the surveillance of Prospero and his spirit. And twelve years before, Antonio had connived at the little-less-than-murder of his brother Prospero and the infant heir to the throne, Miranda, by setting them afloat in a leaky boat. It is a heavy criminal record; and surely it deserves to be treated seriously by a responsible dramatist? But Antonio and Sebastian are treated in a very cursory way in the last scene. Prospero says:

> But you, my brace of lords, were I so minded,
> I here could pluck his highness' frown upon you,
> And justify you traitors. At this time
> I will tell no tales.
>
> *Sebastian: (aside)*   The devil speaks in him.
> *Prospero:* No—
> For you, most wicked sir, whom to call brother
> Would even infect my mouth, I do forgive
> Thy rankest fault—all of them; and require
> My dukedom of thee, which perforce, I know,
> *(V, i, 126-34)*   Thou must restore.

3. *A Study of Shakespeare* (1880), pp. 152-53.

But, again, do we really want to hear Antonio's being given a thorough dressing down at this point in the play, when things are obviously nearing an end and we can think of our way home? The casualness of the treatment of this situation is probably due, not to preposterous magnanimity on the part of Prospero, but to the sensible economy of the dramatist who understands us, his audience, as fully as he does his characters on stage, and probably for the same reason: his imaginative awareness of human beings.

In *All's Well that Ends Well* we may feel that Bertram does not deserve Helena, that he loves her as little toward the end of the play as he did at the beginning. Are we not incredulous, even scornful, of his absurd couplet:

If she, my liege, can make me know this clearly,
I'll love her dearly, ever, ever dearly.   *(V, iii, 316-17)*

All this censure can be justified. And yet it is probably based upon a mistake. Shakespeare's art is really superior to the perceptions of his critics. At this point in the play we have had enough. We are content to allow Bertram to be handed over to his spiritual healer and to agree that all is well because the end is well.

Penitence, contrition, and conversion were, moreover, once a genuine belief of mankind. Religion encouraged the notion, and fiction found it convenient.

Between the saddle and the ground
He mercy sought and mercy found.

Early literature is full of changes of heart, radical repentances of villains. In a post-Freudian world we take a more disillusioned view of human nature. We find it hard to believe, as earlier centuries did, that there can be a complete conversion or reformation. What do we think of Mr. B. in Richardson's *Pamela*, who repents of his wicked designs on the girl and marries her? Our incredulity here is strong, for we fear that Mr. B's change of heart is only skin deep and that he will soon be at his old games again. But in Shakespeare's artistry prompt repentance is a real and credible psychological condition. Proteus, Laertes, Edmund, Iachimo, Leontes, even Caliban, repent and are immediately forgiven. We must grant the same conces-

sion to Angelo and Bertram—and with brevity of words when
the play is taking too much time in ending.

Dramatists and novelists are careful with the naming of their
characters. They give them a great deal of thought. Dickens
used to scour the education lists in order to discover interesting names. I know that one distinguished modern novelist,
who happens also to hold an academic appointment, reads
each new list of examination candidates with excitement, delighted to find useful names for characters in his books.
Shakespeare has many successes, we would all admit. His in-
ventions such as the names of Othello, Ophelia, and Caliban
have a subtle fitness. We applaud the lucky chance that led
him to abandon the historical Oldcastle and to adopt out-
rageously another historical name, the immortal Falstaff.
Shakespeare's success with the ladies' names has been outstanding. Throughout the English-speaking world female in-
fants have, since the middle of the nineteenth century, been
baptized with given names that owed their popularity, and
sometimes their form, to their appearance in Shakespeare's
plays. Viola, Juliet, and Julia began their popular career. Celia,
a form of Cecilia or Cecily, was used as a fanciful name in the
seventeenth and eighteenth centuries, but Shakespeare's use of
it is responsible for its later vogue. Rosalind first appeared in
Thackeray's *The Newcomes* (1854). Beatrice was out of
fashion in the seventeenth and eighteenth centuries and in the
early nineteenth; it then had a revival that doubtless owed
more to Shakespeare than to Dante's Bice de' Portinari. Hermione, pronounced with a long "i", has had its following.
Imogen, probably a misprint for Innogen, has acquired a
romantic charm. The unlucky ladies, Desdemona, Ophelia, and
Cordelia, have understandably been less often heard at the
baptismal font.

Polonius, too, is a successful name, more so than the
Corambis of the earlier play (or of the First Quarto). But, on
reflection, we may have some uneasiness that such should be
the name of the principal minister at the court of Denmark, in
a play that involved the conquest of part of the adjacent kingdom of Poland. In real life, there is no reason why someone
who happened to be named Mr. Britain should not be presi-

dent of the United States, or a Mr. French prime minister of England, or a M. Langlais minister for defense in France. But in fictions we expect things to be a bit more carefully arranged.

Among Falstaff's followers the name Pistol is as outrageous a pun as Falstaff. Corporal Nym has a fascinating etymology. Bardolph (Bardol[l] in the Quartos of *1 Henry IV*) is a stroke of genius, for already in Shakespeare's time the word *bar* was used for that barrier over which drink is served to customers. Appropriately does Bardolph eventually find occupation as a tapster. Having so firmly made the acquaintance of this noxious and entertaining character in the first part of *Henry IV*, with what horror do we listen to the opening words of the second part of the play! A gentlemanly character enters and cries out:

Who keeps the gate here? Ho! Where is the earl?
Porter: What shall I say you are?

To this question the astonishing reply is given:

Tell thou the earl
That the Lord Bardolph doth attend him here.

Has he been raised to the peerage and got rid of his wonderful nose by drinking water?

Porter: His lordship is walked forth into the orchard.
    Please it your honour, knock but at the gate,
    And he himself will answer.
Lord Bardolph: Here comes the earl.
Northumberland: What news, Lord Bardolph?   *(I, i, 1-7)*

We have a sense of relief in the second act when the other Bardolph—the real Bardolph, I am tempted to say—appears, complete with his unextinguishable nose.

Shakespeare seems to be disregarding the petty consequences of these confusions. No artistic explanation is here forthcoming. But sometimes the untidiness of names (in the texts of the plays as we have them) may give some hints of major matters of Shakespeare's artistry. In the first scene of *As You Like It*, indeed in the first few sentences, Orlando mentions an elder brother of his besides Oliver:

My brother Jaques he keeps at school [*that is, university*], and
(I, i, 4) report speaks goldenly of his profit.

We should normally expect Shakespeare to have some purpose
in introducing brother Jaques to the audience thus early. He is
an intellectual, a university man, we observe: one who might
be expected to display "the scholar's melancholy, which is
emulation" (IV, i, 10).

No sooner are we in the Forest of Arden but we are carefully introduced, by detailed description and characterization,
to "the melancholy Jaques" (II, i, 26). This name is repeated
four times, to make sure the audience gets it (ll. 26, 41, 43,
54). Jaques is clearly an intellectual, a university wit. He mor-
alizes the "spectacle" of

>   a poor sequestered stag
> That from the hunter's aim had ta'en a hurt

>   ... into a thousand similes ...
> Thus most invectively he pierceth through
> *(II, i, 33-34,* The body of the country, city, court,
> *45, 58-60)* Yea, and of this our life.

He is left "in this contemplation, . . . commenting Upon the
sobbing deer"; and "in these sullen fits . . . he's full of matter"
(ll. 64-68). All this would fit very well the Jaques, bred at the
university, the second son of Sir Rowland de Boys, whom the
old Duke (we have been carefully told by Rosalind) loved as
his son and whom the usurping Duke ever found his enemy.
But no relationship to Orlando is mentioned, and it soon becomes clear that this is quite a different Jaques; and when
Orlando and Jaques do have a conversation (III, ii, 268-312)
they are newly acquainted; and a certain amount of rather tart
banter is indulged between "good Signor Love" and "good
Monsieur Melancholy" (ll. 310-12). (Some of this banter could
originally have been fraternal, I suppose.) Eventually the
middle brother of Oliver and Orlando does enter (V, iv, 157)
and announces himself:

> Let me have audience for a word or two.
> I am the second son of old Sir Rowland,
> That bring these tidings to this fair assembly.

In the Folio (our only text) his name is not mentioned. The stage direction here merely says *"Enter Second Brother"* and the speech heading *"2. Bro."*.

What has happened? It shows a certain carelessness and an invitation to confusion to have two characters in the play with, pointlessly, the same name. The occurrence of the two Jaques (who would mislead an audience if it were quick and perceptive enough) presumably indicates some change of plan upon Shakespeare's part: the *three* brothers were, at first, intended to be major characters in the play, but for some reason Shakespeare removed Jaques's family relationship. Perhaps we have a glimpse of Shakespeare's artistry if we ask why.

First, everybody at the court seems to know where the banished Duke is:

> They say he is already in the forest of Arden, and a many merry men with him; and there they live like the old Robin Hood of England. They say many young gentlemen flock to him every day . . . *(I, i, 120-24)*

When Rosalind is banished, Celia proposes to accompany her. "Why, whither shall we go? " asks Rosalind; and Celia replies:

> To seek my uncle in the forest of Arden. *(I, iii, 108-9)*

The usurping Duke is then mistakenly told that Orlando accompanied Rosalind and Celia in their escape. The audience knows this to be untrue: the girls are alone, apart from Touchstone, and that is why Rosalind assumes male attire. But the Duke's mistake serves to reintroduce Orlando's brother, Oliver; to provide an excuse for exiling Orlando, too; and then for sending Oliver in pursuit of him. It would be natural to arrange for Orlando, when he escapes Oliver's plots, to set out for Arden to join the other "many young gentlemen" who flock there every day (among whom we might have expected to find his other brother, called Jaques). But Orlando is shown as knowing nothing of this. He and Adam arrive in the Forest of Arden by accident, it seems. He rushes in upon the Duke's outdoor banquet, with drawn sword; and is amazed at his civil reception:

> Speak you so gently? Pardon me, I pray you.
> I thought that all things had been savage here. *(II, vii, 106-7)*

There is no recognition of the brothers. Jaques responds to Orlando's threats with a sardonic pun (presumably plucking a grape from the table and eating it):

(l. 100) An you will not be answered with reason, I must die

Jaques shortly afterward delivers his great set piece on the Seven Ages of Man, regardless of any brotherly relation to Orlando. Orlando sits down to the meal, which is accompanied by a song about "benefits forgot" and "friend remembered not." He has no idea into whose company he has fallen until the Duke tells him.

But is not this the brilliant theatrical moment toward which Shakespeare has been working, which justifies the suppression of the Jaques relationship and the absurdity of Orlando's not knowing what is happening in the Forest of Arden? We have seen the beginning of Orlando's love for Rosalind and of Rosalind's for Orlando. We have seen him respond to the usurping Duke's insults by boldly asserting

I am more proud to be Sir Rowland's son,
His youngest son, and would not change that calling
(I, ii, 245-47) To be adopted heir to Frederick.

We know that he is the young giant-quelling hero, the soul of honor, who is destined to win the Princess. And now he stands before the Duke, the father of his beloved, and we watch the revelation:

If that you were the good Sir Rowland's son,
As you have whispered faithfully you were,
And as mine eye doth his effigies witness
Most truly limned and living in your face,
Be truly welcome hither. I am the Duke
That loved your father.

And Orlando kneels in fealty to his rightful liege, kissing his hand or offering his sword for the oath of allegiance. The Duke quietly leads him off the stage.

(II, vii, 191-   The residue of your fortune,
97)   Go to my cave and tell me.

Usually the needs of character and of the story determine

Shakespeare's choice of words. It was Pope's compliment to Shakespeare that

His *Characters* are so much Nature her self, that 'tis a sort of injury to call them by so distant a name as Copies of her. . . . Every single character in *Shakespeare* is as much an Individual, as those in Life itself. . . . To this life and variety of Character, we must add the wonderful Preservation of it; which is such throughout his plays, that had all the Speeches been printed without the very names of the Persons, I believe one might have apply'd them with certainty to every speaker.[4]

This may be a trifle bardolatrous in Pope. We must admit that there are occasions when the words come before the dramatic conception or have a life independent of it. And occasionally Shakespeare may let the character go hang if he is intent on certain scenic effects. Partly this is because authors do become fascinated by their fictional characters. They have confessed to their weakness in this respect and described the struggles they have undergone in subduing these characters to the demands of the plot. Little Paul Dombey is one of Dicken's shrewdest and most captivating creations. The major purposes of Dickens in *Dombey and Son* compelled him to let little Paul die half-way through the novel. It was painful to Dickens. And he could not forget it.

When I am reminded by any chance of what it was that the waves were always saying, my remembrance wanders for a whole winter night about the streets of Paris—as I restlessly did with a heavy heart, on the night when I had written the chapter in which my little friend and I parted company.[5]

A less conscientious artist than Dickens might perhaps have been prepared to damage his plot rather than abandon a successful piece of characterization. The suspicion has been with us for a long time that Shakespeare was quite capable of letting a successful bit of virtuoso characterization, such as Shylock, run away with him. Perhaps in the fourth act of *The Merchant of Venice* he had not controlled his artistic energies

4. *Eighteenth Century Essays on Shakespeare*, ed. D. Nichol Smith, 2d ed. (Oxford, 1963), p. 45.
5. Preface to *Dombey and Son.*

adequately. Somehow he must get the audience back into the original or intended mood of the play. And Shakespeare knows what he can do with his audience.

We are tolerant when that rather commonplace young man Lorenzo (hitherto a mercenary-minded, daughter-stealing Venetian) asks us to observe

> How sweet the moonlight sleeps upon this bank.
> Here will we sit and let the sounds of music
> Creep in our ears. Soft stillness and the night
> *(V, i, 54-57)* Become the touches of sweet harmony.

After all, Jessica and Lorenzo are new lovers; and we delight to hear the romantic nonsense that new lovers articulate to each other.

(l. 69) I am never merry when I hear sweet music

observes Jessica, inviting Lorenzo to give her a clever explanation, and fill her with admiration for his hitherto unsuspected and unrevealed intellectual powers. "The reason is," he begins—well, we need not remind ourselves what his reason is— some Neoplatonic twaddle, no doubt. We are not in a censorious mood. We are not going to be so stupid as to complain about Shakespeare's "inconsistency of characterization" in dealing with Lorenzo. We are glad to be in the moonlight with the lovers and the music; back in Belmont after all the terrors and excitements of the Venetian lawcourts; back where a happy Christian-Jewish marriage mollifies the bitterness of the Christian-Jewish conflict of the fourth act.

In noticing, and trying to explain, discrepancies of characterization in the plays, we must take into consideration, too, what a dynamic actor can do to a thin, ambiguous, or contradictory part. He can make homogeneous, by the continuity of his personality, a part that verbally may seem inconsistent. He can so control the audience's reactions, so dominate them by what he, with his real personality or with an assumed one, gives to the role, that the new dimension of realization unifies the speeches into a consistent "character."

But does Shakespeare, owing to his lifelong involvement in theater business, rely too much upon this? He may go near the edge sometimes. But, with the striking exceptions of *The*

Comedy of Errors and *The Winter's Tale*, he never disguises the plot from the audience. He always takes them into his confidence as regards the progress of events and the developing action. It is probable, therefore, that he can take risks with the characters; that, having carefully established a personality of a particular kind in the play, he can proceed to give it passages of poetry that are definitely not "in character."

It is perplexing that several of Shakespeare's great passages of poetry are not organic, or at least not obviously so. At times, certainly, he writes poetical "set pieces" that are splendidly relevant. There are many in *Hamlet*, *Othello*, *King Lear*, and *The Tempest*, for example. But some highly wrought passages are not easily spoken by the actor who has had to build up the "character" from the action of the play. In the case of the early plays this apparent defect is sometimes attributed to Shakespeare's inexperience. In *Richard III*, for example, the hateful murderer, James Tyrrel, gives the audience a touching account of the two little princes in the Tower of London:

Dighton and Forrest, whom I did suborn
To do this piece of ruthful butchery,
Albeit they were fleshed villains, bloody dogs,
Melting with tenderness and mild compassion,
Wept like to children in their death's sad story.
"O, thus," quoth Dighton, "lay the gentle babes."
"Thus, thus," quoth Forrest, "girdling one another
Within their alablaster innocent arms.
Their lips were four red roses on a stalk,
Which in their summer beauty kissed each other.
A book of prayers on their pillow lay;
Which once," quoth Forrest "almost changed my mind.
But, O, the devil"—there the villain stopped;
When Dighton thus told on: "We smotherèd
The most replenishèd sweet work of nature
That from the prime creation e'er she framed." *(IV, iii, 4-19)*

The Queen Mab speech in *Romeo and Juliet* has to be spoken by Mercutio. It is a splendid piece of writing, an opportunity for a display of his virtuosity by the actor. Yet it is not altogether clear that it fits the "character" of Mercutio as it is built up in other parts of the play. Sensitive literary critics have to get to work to explain just how appropriate it is for

Mercutio to speak the lines. The director ensures that the actor who plays Mercutio has the dynamism to dominate the audience and put the speech over.

But this failure to make some of his great poetical passages organic remains, perhaps, with Shakespeare in his maturity. The storm scene in *Julius Caesar* is written with great splendor and intensity:

Are not you moved, when all the sway of earth
Shakes like a thing unfirm? O Cicero,
I have seen tempests, when the scolding winds
Have rived the knotty oaks, and I have seen
The ambitious ocean swell and rage and foam,
To be exalted with the threatening clouds;
But never till tonight, never till now,
Did I go through a tempest dropping fire.
Either there is a civil strife in heaven,
Or else the world, too saucy with the gods,
Incenses them to send destruction . . .
                    When these prodigies
Do so conjointly meet, let not men say
"These are their reasons, they are natural,"
(I, iii, 3-13,   For, I believe, they are portentous things
28-32)   Unto the climate that they point upon.

But the speaker of these lines, Casca, has been built up in the previous scene of the play as a blunt, matter-of-fact, fellow; a skeptic; one who is not easily rattled. Are these superstitious fears really appropriate to his character? Perhaps the quasi-psychologists here leap forward and explain how "true to human nature" it is, this trait of romantic superstition and terror in a personality who is outwardly phlegmatic and imperturbable. Well, you have to tell that to the actor who has been entrusted with Casca; and perhaps he can play it, with the unification that *his* personality provides, so that the audience does not become aware of any discrepancy or inconsistency. Nevertheless we can have sympathy with those critics who think that something has gone wrong with our text of the play here: that the attribution of these speeches to Casca is due to some economy of casting in the playhouse and that the scene was built up by Shakespeare around an entirely different (and new) character.

It is this situation that makes it difficult to be fair to Shakespeare's artistry: we can feel little confidence in the integrity of the texts of the plays. We can never know, for the great majority of plays, how far the texts we possess represent cut versions of Shakespeare's fuller intentions. In a few cases we do possess two texts of a play (*Romeo and Juliet, Hamlet, King Lear, The Merry Wives of Windsor, Henry V, Othello*). Here the evidence for variable cutting is strong. In order to prepare a text of *Hamlet* we add the Quarto lines missing from the Folio and the Folio lines missing from the Quarto, and this enables us to make the vulgate text of nearly four thousand lines. But it is reasonable to suppose that, when two persons independently cut the text of a play for the stage, they would occasionally both decide, independently, to cut the same passage. If the Folio cutter and the Quarto cutter of *Hamlet* happened to cut the same passage — as seems quite likely — then that passage of Shakespeare's play is lost forever.

What cutting lies behind the texts of plays that exist in only one form (*Macbeth* or *The Two Gentlemen of Verona*, to take two notorious examples), who can possibly say? Our discussions of Shakespeare's artistry must, therefore, be made uncertain by our lack of confidence in our actually possessing the works of art, in their completeness, on which we exercise our critical perceptions.

There is another economical but dangerous device on which Shakespeare relies in plays on historical themes: taking for granted the knowledge that the audience already possesses of the character. The expectations of the audience are very important, for example in *Julius Caesar*. Shakespeare does not need to represent in the play the greatness of Caesar. All he needs to do is to add to or modify the impressions the audience have of him. Hence we may feel, merely from the text, that the play is unsympathetic to Caesar. But Caesar has an imaginative existence outside the play. The persons in *Julius Caesar* talk about him as "the foremost man of all this world," one who "doth bestride the narrow world / Like a Colossus." Shakespeare does not need to show this, because the estimate of Caesar's greatness is one that the audience already shares with the personages in the play. Shakespeare is economical. He knows what he can take for granted. He only needs to indicate the little traits and foibles, susceptibility to flattery, and so on, that humanize the greatest man in history.

In *Antony and Cleopatra* the problem is less serious because Shakespeare's assumptions about the two lovers (which represent the viewpoint of his contemporaries) were not so very different from ours. We do not have to correct our assumptions in order to understand the play, as we do have to correct them in order to understand *Julius Caesar*. Still, there are assumptions about the character of Cleopatra that Shakespeare can take for granted. Everyone knows that Cleopatra was the most fascinating woman in the world, the most wonderful of lovers, the conqueror of Julius Caesar as well as Mark Antony. He does not have to show this in the action of the play; it would be superfluous. He can take all that for granted in the audience's reactions, and spend his dramatic time in adding to it; in showing the woman's tantrums rather than those wonders of love — which would be difficult, anyway, for a boy player to represent; we should not expect Shakespeare to be so unwise as to try and show us

Some squeaking Cleopatra boy [her] greatness
(V, ii, 220-21) I'the posture of a whore

We need not be surprised that (as some critics have pointed out) the behavior of Cleopatra in the play, at least in the first four acts, does not quite correspond with the way in which some of the others talk about her. It is Enobarbus, the shrewd and disillusioned soldier, whom Shakespeare chooses as the mouthpiece of her praise.

Age cannot wither her, nor custom stale
Her infinite variety. Other women cloy
The appetites they feed. But she makes hungry
Where most she satisfies. For vilest things
Become themselves in her; that the holy priests
(II, ii, 240-45) Bless her when she is riggish.

There is surely no inconsistency of character-drawing between this poetical evocation and, say, the scenes in which she strikes and interrogates the messenger who brings news of Antony's marriage to Octavia (II, v and III, iii). Shakespeare is adding certain episodes and certain plausible traits of character to the general idea we have of Cleopatra (which is much the same as the idea held by the personages in the play, as is evidenced by the way they talk about her). It all together adds up to a character that is consistent with her conduct in the fifth act, where she rises to sublime heights.

As a dramaturgical device a reliance upon the audience's extradramatic expectations is economical and useful. There is, of course, a varying reliance on these expectations. In the case of some of the ancient figures, such as Julius Caesar and Cleopatra, there is a great deal of reliance on what the audience knows about the character. So is there in *Richard III*, where in the last scene Shakespeare has the audacity to bring Queen Elizabeth's grandfather onto the stage. In the case of Coriolanus there is practically no reliance on extradramatic knowledge at all—every detail of Coriolanus's character is carefully built up, step by step, with admirable artistic conscience.

The difficulty is that we may nowadays have quite different stereotyped ideas about historical figures. Cleopatra may still be the eternal charmer. But Julius Caesar has diminished in stature; for the Roman Empire and its emperors do not have the same importance in the total history of our world and in our educational system. Sometimes our historical clichés are seriously damaging in dealing with some of Shakespeare's characters. Consider Joan of Arc. The heroic maid rehabilitated and canonized by the Roman church and recreated by Bernard Shaw has conditioned us in such a way that the vile creature in *Henry VI*, the witch who gives her blood to be drunk by fiends, the coward, cheat, and liar of the English chronicles, has become intolerable. We bring audience expectations to Joan of Arc that destroy any possibility of our responding with simplicity to the characterization in Shakespeare's play.

Our difficulties are largely a consequence of Shakespeare's kind of artistry: in many cases his method of characterization is not represented by the words on the page or in the mouth of the actor. It dangerously relies on circumstance outside the work of art. We cannot assess Julius Caesar's role in the play by meditating on the one hundred fifty lines he speaks.

Modern literary criticism desiderates works of art that have an organic unity; in which all the parts are relevant to the whole; in which characterization, imagery, thematic development or balance, bind the work of art together as a well-concatenated object. Such is the ideal work of art upon which the critic most enjoys employing his ingenuity, his sensitivity, his intelligence. The reaction against the "disintegration" of Shakespeare has led to a powerful integration of Shakespeare. Not only has the concept of "organic unity" been given a new lease of critical life; it has been strengthened by such notions as "sustained imagery" and "thematic structure." Individual plays have been given a coherence or cohesion of parts, hitherto unsuspected.

Nevertheless, in my judgment, sometimes Shakespeare is not writing so "good" a play as his modern critics seem to be concerned with. Shakespeare is not writing nearly so carefully or alertly as some of our sensitive literary analysts try to demonstrate. The nature of Shakespeare's artistry deserves a judicious enquiry more detached from our favorite aesthetic theories or assumptions. His art does not fit well into some characteristic twentieth-century views on what a great work of art should be. Sometimes it does, but not always. Simple answers such as: "Shakespeare was a playwright providing popular entertainment. He knew he could get away with anything on the stage" are of little value. Yes, sometimes he does get away with it, but not always. Impatient or irritable responses—that the great Shakespeare does not worry about such trifles and that they will never be noticed in the theater—are only another aspect of the theory that we can swallow anything from our national institution. To say that in the theater hardly anybody cares about the thousands of little artistic flaws in the plays—they do not matter—is not a compliment to Shakespeare. One could equally well say that in the theater hardly anybody cares about the thousands of little artistic subtleties in the plays, therefore they do not matter. A more flexible and varied approach to Shakespeare's artistry seems necessary. There is no general theory of dramatic art that can cover all his successes and (apparent) failures or lapses. We can admit that Shakespeare was a busy man of the theater, living the somewhat dizzy life of theater folk, writing a million or more of words of high-quality poetry in twenty years. We must not exclude the probability that Shakespeare could be occasionally careless. But his apparent negligences may at times be rational economies of art: I have suggested that we should take note of his frugality in artistic effort: of the relaxed attention of the audience at the end of the plays; of his use of extra-dramatic expectations by the audience to supplement characterization, so that the audience contributes something that is not in the play; of his confidence in the dynamism of the actor who can dominate an audience and (by contributing his own artistic and human personality) make homogenous what seems, when we consider merely the words on the page, discrepant or contradictory; of his bold willingness sometimes to abandon certain developments of plot or to suspend characterization, because of the needs of more important artistic questions in the play. And in all such considerations there must be, I admit, a conviction that, when it comes to the artistic crisis, Shakespeare can get away with it. Since there is scarcely a play of Shakespeare that does not show flaws, a candid and conscientious consideration of the instances of Shakespeare's lack of care (whether apparent or real, whether major or trivial) could give us, I believe, a better awareness of Shakespeare at work.

All's Well with Lafew

James G. McManaway

6

Like the Foucault pendulum that astronomers use to demonstrate the diurnal movement of the earth, the pendulum of
Shakespeare criticism moves with the passing years in various
directions. Now it is in the direction of character analysis; then
it concerns itself with the beauties of Shakespeare; at another
time, critics have read the plays for their ethical and religious
preachments. Now and again, the pendulum has been given,
temporarily, an aberrant movement, as when Walter Whiter in
1794 showed the way to the recognition and study of Shakespeare's imagery, only to find that no one else would see his
new path, much less follow it.

Perhaps the earliest example of aberrant criticism is in John
Dryden's reference to Mercutio in 1672. In his "Defence of the
Epilogue," included in part two of *The Conquest of Granada*,
Dryden compares the "somewhat . . . ill-bred and clownish"
wit of the past age with the courtly wit of the Restoration
period and by way of illustration writes:

Shakespeare showed the best of his skill in his Mercutio; and
he said himself, that he was forced to kill him in the third act,
to prevent being killed by him.

Then he adds, with a certain condescension:

But, for my part, I see nothing in him but what was so exceedingly harmless, that he might have lived to the end of the
play, and died in his bed, without offence to any man.[1]

Dryden's intention was to write only of the wit in Mercutio's

---

1. W. P. Ker, ed., *Essays of John Dryden*, 1 (Oxford: Oxford University Press, 1900):174.

lines, and it was to this subject that Dr. Johnson directed his first remarks:

> Nor do I doubt the ability of Shakespeare to have continued [Mercutio's] existence though some of his sallies are perhaps out of the reach of Dryden; whose genius was not very fertile of merriment, nor ductile to humour.

Then Johnson introduced a new element:

> Mercutio's wit, gaiety, and courage, will always procure him friends that wish him a longer life; but his death is not precipitated, he has lived out the term allotted to him in the construction of the play.[2]

Echoing and amplifying Johnson's opinion, Samuel Taylor Coleridge summed up Mercutio thus:

> By his loss it was contrived that the whole catastrophe of the tragedy should be brought about.

Then he added:

> I say this in answer to an observation by Dryden (to which indeed Dr. Johnson has fully replied) that Shakespeare having carried the part of Mercutio as far as he could, till his genius was exhausted, had killed him in the third Act, to get him out of the way. What shallow nonsense! As I have remarked, upon the death of Mercutio the whole catastrophe depends; it is produced by it. . . . Had not Mercutio been rendered so amiable and so interesting, we could not have felt so strongly the necessity for Romeo's interference.[3]

The consideration of Mercutio is now on wholly different ground from that stated in Dryden's anecdote. It is no longer a question of wit but of function. For the most part, however, commentators were no more inclined to follow the path suggested by Coleridge than that of Walter Whiter. In consequence, there has been general neglect of what may be called the two-dimensional characters that play minor roles, and those that have received attention have often been misinterpreted.

2. Arthur Sherbo, ed., *Johnson on Shakespeare*, vol. 8 of *The Yale Johnson* (New Haven: Yale University Press, 1968), pp. 956-57.

3. T. M. Raysor, ed., *Coleridge's Shakespearean Criticism*, 2 (London: Constable, 1930): 132, 133.

Not even major characters have escaped calumny. In the introduction to his edition of *The Merchant of Venice*,[4] Sir Arthur Quiller-Couch launched an all-out attack on Bassanio and his Venetian friends, who—barring Antonio—are, every one of them, "either a 'wastrel' or a 'rotter' or both." "But let us consider this conquering hero, Bassanio," writes Q.

When first we meet him he is in debt, a condition on which—having to confess it because he wants to borrow more money—he expends some very choice diction.

>   "'Tis not unknown to you, Antonio,"

(no, certainly it was not!)

>   "How much I have disabled mine estate,
>   By something showing a more swelling port
>   Than my faint means could grant continuance. . . ."

That may be a mighty fine way of saying that you have chosen to live beyond your income; but, Shakespeare or no Shakespeare, if Shakespeare means us to hold Bassanio for an honest fellow, it is mighty poor poetry. For poetry, like honest men, looks things in the face, and does not ransack its wardrobe to clothe what is naturally unpoetical. . . .

[Bassanio] goes on to say that he is not repining; his chief anxiety is to pay everybody, and

>   "to you, Antonio,
>   I owe the most in money and in love,"

and thereupon counts on more love to extract more money. . . . And what is Bassanio's project? To borrow three thousand ducats to equip himself to go off and hunt an heiress in Belmont. . . .

He gets the money, of course, equips himself lavishly, and arrives at Belmont; . . . I suppose that, while character weighs in drama, if one thing be more certain than another it is that a predatory young gentleman such as Bassanio would *not* have chosen the leaden casket.

By omission, I have diminished and considerably simplified Q's arraignment of Bassanio.

Moved by Q's eloquence and guided by his scorn, more than one director has produced *The Merchant of Venice* in such a way as to oppose a profligate Venetian society to the

---

4. *New Shakespeare* (Cambridge: Cambridge University Press, 1926), pp. xxiii ff.

idyllic household in Belmont and has thus added credibility to the presentation of Shylock as a racial martyr. More than once the friendship of Antonio and Bassanio has even been given a strong homosexual coloring.

The theatrical perversions of the play are hardly more culpable than Quiller-Couch's denigration of Bassanio. As a scholar and editor he should have read C. R. Baskervill's "Bassanio as an Ideal Lover,"[5] published three years before the New Shakespeare *Merchant*. And even without knowledge of that essay he should have heeded the ample hints Shakespeare gives of Bassanio's worth. The hero of this romantic comedy is named twice in Venice in the first scene of the play: "Here comes Bassanio, your most noble kinsman," and later, "My Lord Bassanio." And he has not been forgotten in Belmont.

Nerissa: Do you not remember, lady, in your father's time, a Venetian, a scholar and a soldier, that came hither in company of the Marquis of Montferrat?
Portia: Yes, yes, it was Bassanio;

then, checking her impetuosity,

                                        as I think, so was he call'd.
Nerissa must not guess the vividness of Portia's memories.

Nerissa: True, madam; he, of all the men that ever my foolish eyes look'd upon, was the best deserving a fair lady.
Portia: I remember him well, and I remember him worthy of
(I, ii, 100-108)   thy praise. . . .[6]

Provided for his quest, Bassanio arrives at Belmont just as the luckless Arragon is being dismissed. A servant enters to Portia:

Servant: Madam, there is alighted at your gate
A young Venetian, one that comes before
To signify th'approaching of his lord,
From whom he bringeth sensible regreets;
To wit, besides commends and courteous breath,
Gifts of rich value. Yet I have not seen

5. *The Manly Anniversary Studies in Language and Literature* (Chicago: University of Chicago Press, 1923), pp. 90-103.
6. Quotations from Shakespeare are from *The Complete Works*, ed. Peter Alexander (London and Glasgow: Collins, 1951).

So likely an ambassador of love. . . .
Portia: . . . Come, come, Nerissa, for I long to see
Quick Cupid's post that comes so mannerly.
Nerissa: Bassanio, Lord Love, if thy will it be!

(II, ix, 86-92, 99-101)

Despite Portia's pleas that he defer the choice of caskets "some month or two" (III, i, 9), Bassanio's love is so great and so impatient that he lives upon the rack; and so, with Portia's confession of her love echoing in his ears, he confronts the caskets. There is no need to rehearse for this gathering Baskervill's symbolic and philosophical interpretation of Bassanio's reasoning and choice—which, you will recall, has nothing to do with dinning rhymes that sound like *lead*.

After the lady has been won, there is time for only one kiss before Salerio arrives with the news that Antonio's life is forfeit. Instantly the marriage ceremony is performed, and Portia sends Bassanio with gold and her blessing to ransom Antonio. Lorenzo then praises Portia for her "noble and a true conceit Of [the] god-like amity" that exists between Antonio and Bassanio.

There is one last proof of Bassanio's worth. Back at Belmont again, Antonio intervenes in the wrangling about the rings.

I once did lend my body for his wealth,
Which, but for him that had your husband's ring,
Had quite miscarried; I dare be bound again,
My soul upon the forfeit, that your lord
Will never more break faith advisedly.

(V, i, 249-53)

Now if we really believe that "greater love hath no man than this, that a man lay down his life for his friends" (John 15:13), then a man capable of inspiring such sacrificial love deserves better than to be called a "wastrel" and a "rotter."

The detailing of some of the evidence is not intended as a defense of Bassanio, but as an indication of the kind of clues that Shakespeare gives habitually to the evaluation and interpretation of characters of more than nominal importance— clues that commentators ignore to their peril.

As was suggested earlier, it is characters in the middle group, neither high nor low, that suffer most frequently from neglect or misinterpretation. Often their value is chiefly functional: they represent a norm of conduct or an attitude by which to measure the actions and utterances of their betters. Enobarbus comes to mind as such a character. He fares better than most by having been given such prominence that there is genuine concern for him at his death. In the exotic Egyptian setting, he seems to some critics to stand uncompromisingly for Roman values, both private and public. Professor Virgil Whitaker goes somewhat beyond this when, in writing of a scene, he states that Enobarbus "serves throughout the play as the voice of reason."[7] It can be argued, I think, that Enobarbus has a more complex function. As Antony's loyal friend and follower, he warns Lepidus at the meeting of the triumvirs that he will not advise Antony to use "soft and gentle speech"; instead, he will

> entreat him
> To answer like himself. If Caesar move him,
> Let Antony look over Caesar's head
> *(II, ii, 3-6)* And speak as loud as Mars.

Speaking only half in jest, he can give sound advice, as when he warns almost prophetically that Antony's intended departure for Rome will kill all their women.

> Under a compelling occasion, let women die. It were pity to
> cast them away for nothing, though between them and a great
> *(I, ii, 134-36)* cause they should be esteemed nothing.

On occasion, he is the blunt soldier. "That truth should be silent, I had almost forgot," he tells Antony (II, ii, 112), when the triumvirs are trying with fine words to smooth over their animosities so as to unite against Pompey.

There can be no questioning of the military acumen of Enobarbus. In the face of Cleopatra's wrath, he opposes her intended presence at the battle of Actium, suggesting in an aside that if both stallions and mares are to be ridden into battle the mares, doubly ridden, will be more hotly pursued than the enemy. But in this decision about strategy, as on other occasions, his wisdom serves only to expose the folly of Antony.

7. *Shakespeare's Use of Learning* (San Marino, California: Henry E. Huntington Library, 1953), p. 316.

Two incidents call for further comment, and I shall consider them in reverse order. Loyal as Enobarbus was to Antony, there came a time when disgust over Antony's deterioration forced him to quit the general he could no longer respect. Common sense told him that

The loyalty well held to fools does make
Our faith mere folly. Yet he that can endure
To follow with allegiance a fall'n lord
Does conquer him that did his master conquer
And earns a place i' th' story.

(III, xiii, 42-46)

Shortly after this, he abandoned Antony. Almost he had attained to wisdom, but not quite. When Antony sent all of Enobarbus's treasure after him, that display of generosity quite overwhelmed him, and in shame and contrition his heart burst. For all his hard Roman practicality, his wisdom had fallen short of that of King Lear's Fool.

That sir which serves and seeks for gain,
    And follows but for form,
Will pack when it begins to rain,
    And leave thee in the storm.
But I will tarry; the fool will stay
    And let the wise man fly.
The knave turns fool that runs away;
    The fool no knave, perdy.

(II, iv, 79-86)

About the death of Enobarbus, the only adverse criticism of consequence is that Shakespeare encouraged too much audience identification with the repentant soldier. But it can be argued that Enobarbus had drawn "a circle premature" and paid no more than the just penalty of being less wise than Lear's Fool. It may also be pointed out that in the darkening picture of Antony in decline, Shakespeare has here painted one bright stroke of Antony's magnanimity.

The earlier incident requiring discussion is the description of Cleopatra when she and Antony first met. You remember the occasion. Antony and his retinue are in Rome, and the adherents of Octavius and Pompey are trying to give them a hard time. They lose no opportunity to ask questions about Egypt, the land of gold and mystery, which had inspired travelers' tales since Theophrastus. Half filled with genuine curios-

ity and half with malice, they inquire about such fabulous
things as Egypt's pyramids and monster-spawning Nile. The
information Antony gives Lepidus about crocodiles is, I think,
the only example of Roman humor in the play. The questions
asked Enobarbus, and even some of Pompey's remarks to
Antony, are sharply barbed, appearing to praise while actually
disparaging Cleopatra, so as to put Antony and Enobarbus on
the defensive.

Thus, Agrippa to Enobarbus:

> Royal wench!
> She made great Caesar lay his sword to bed.
> *(II, ii, 230-32)* He ploughed her, and she cropp'd.

In more exalted society, Pompey's remarks to Antony go
swiftly from food to women:

> *Pompey:* But, first or last, your fine Egyptian cookery
>   Shall have the fame. I have heard that Julius Caesar
>   Grew fat with feasting there.
> *Antony:* You have heard much.
> *Pompey:* I have fair meanings, sir.
> *Antony:*   And fair words to them.
> *Pompey:* Then so much I have heard;
>   And I have heard Apollodorus carried—
> *Enobarbus:*   No more of that: He did so.
> *Pompey:* What, I pray you?
> *(II, vi, 63-70)* *Enobarbus:* A certain queen to Caesar in a mattress.

Now this bald statement of fact by Antony's second in command was good strategy; it might also be called truth in adver-
tising.

So with Enobarbus's lines about Cleopatra at Cydnus. What
is she like, this dame, the Romans want to know.

> The barge she sat in, like a burnish'd throne,
> Burn'd on the water. The poop was beaten gold;
> *(II, ii, 195-97)* Purple the sails.

In sum, Cleopatra "did make defect perfection" (II, ii, 235).
For most readers, this is Cleopatra to the life. But there are a
few who insist that this is all lies, a hoax perpetrated upon the
Romans and upon us. You may take your choice of interpreta-

tions. For my part, I can find no other speech by Enobarbus that is not reason and truth. The Cydnus passage is the grudging concession of a hard-bitten warrior—a vivid memory retained across the years in which Cleopatra has borne children to Antony—that there are more things in heaven and earth than are dreamt of in Roman philosophy. It is to be accepted as truth because it is Enobarbus who speaks it and because Shakespeare at the height of his powers did not make the mistake of letting a functional character like Enobarbus talk out of both sides of his mouth.

Along with Kent and the Fool in *King Lear* and Menenius Agrippa in *Coriolanus*, Enobarbus is what Professor Whitaker has called a chorus character, introduced to underscore the fall of the hero.[8]

Now at last let us consider the character whose name I have taken liberties with in the title of this essay. He is Lafew, in *All's Well That Ends Well*, described in the list of *dramatis personae* of the First Folio as "an old Lord." Editors and critics scarcely mention him. W. W. Lawrence, for example, notes only that he is one of Shakespeare's additions to the story,[9] a fact that in itself should alert us to his possible importance. The New Arden editor, Dr. G. K. Hunter, writes that "The wisdom of the King, the Countess, and Lafew shows in their tolerance and mellow grace. . . ." and adds that "their geniality springs from their humbled wisdom."[10] The most forthright and generous in appraisal of the man is Professor Josephine Waters Bennett:

Lafew is a wonderful study of a truly noble man, so entirely in command of himself that he always sees the need of the moment and attends to it, friend of the Countess, of Helena, of Bertram, of the King, and even friend to Parolles in his need. He is an experienced courtier and true gentleman who can jest his King into good humor or bandy words with Parolles, comfort the Countess, smooth Helena's way to the King,

8. Ibid., p. 247.

9. *Shakespeare's Problem Comedies* (New York: Macmillan, 1931), p. 40.

10. *All's Well That Ends Well*, ed. G. K. Hunter, New Arden Shakespeare (London: Methuen, 1959), p. xxxvii.

or make Bertram's peace with him. He is everything that a man ought to be.[11]

On the stage, Lafew—like the King of France and the Countess of Rossillion—has had his ups and downs. In the middle of the eighteenth century, "Berry's Lafeu [at Drury Lane] was the true portrait of a choleric old man and a humourist."[12] The suspicion that the role was treated as a comic part is increased by Charles Lamb's remarks about Joseph Munden, who played Lafew in Charles Kean's production at Drury Lane in 1811.

He, and he alone, literally makes faces; applied to any other person, the phrase is a mere figure, denoting certain modifications of the human countenance. . . . But in the grand grotesque of farce, Munden stands out as all single and unaccompanied as Hogarth. . . . Can any man *wonder* like he does?[13]

Professor Price conjectures that Munden might have found it easy to be compassionate to Parolles. "While in similar straits as a young man, Munden had passed himself off as a soldier in order to obtain supper and bed from a military billet."[14]

In one production, that of Robert Atkins, Lafew—played not surprisingly by Atkins himself—was the central character of the play.[15]

When *All's Well* was received at the Shakespeare Memorial Theatre in 1933, a "Mr. Stanley Howlett [played] Lafew with a distinction that made it a pleasure to watch [him]. Mr. Howlett made it clear that Lafew, though a humorous old gentleman (humorous in both the Elizabethan and the modern senses of the word) was a gentleman and not a buffoon."[16] In 1953-54, Michael Benthall may have remembered that in his

11. "New Techniques of Comedy in *All's Well That Ends Well*," *Shakespeare Quarterly* 18 (1967): 345.

12. Thomas Davies, *Dramatic Miscellanies* (1784), cited in Joseph G. Price, *The Unfortunate Comedy: A Study of* All's Well That Ends Well *and the Critics* (Toronto: University of Toronto Press, 1968), p. 8.

13. Cited in Price, *The Unfortunate Comedy*, p. 32.

14. Ibid., p. 175, n. 3, citing *Oxberry's Dramatic Biography*, n.s., 2:75.

15. Ibid., p. 82, citing Gordon Crosse, *Shakespearean Playgoing, 1890-1952* (London: Mowbray, 1953), p. 49.

16. Crosse, *Shakespearean Playgoing*, p. 82.

copy of the Second Folio King Charles I wrote in the word *Parolles* as the title of the play (in the same way that he had renamed *Much Ado* as *Benedick and Betteris*). In any case, in that season in Stratford-upon-Avon, audiences saw "the story of Helena and Bertram . . . given the remoteness of a fairy-tale, or at least of the medieval fabliau from which Shakespeare took it."[17] The King and the Countess were made weakly ludicrous or rheumatically awkward, and Lafew was a bumbling comic.

It is against this kind of misrepresentation of Shakespeare that I protest, basing my case on the evidence Shakespeare presents so carefully and generously. Writing of the production of *All's Well* at Stratford in 1953-54, Mr. Richard David says that

Michael Benthall resorted to all the most disreputable tricks of the trade—drastic cutting, transposing, the masking of awkward speeches with music or outrageous buffoonery.

And he continues:

Yet it was not only in spite of these tricks but partly because of them that the producer was able to offer a coherent, convincing, and, as far as I know, a new view of Shakespeare's play, *at least to those who are prepared to allow that in theatrical affairs the end may justify the means.*[18]

I protest that, even in theatrical affairs, the end does not necessarily justify the means. Directors and producers—and the theatrical reviewers who countenance them—that invert, turn inside out, or impose their own conception of a play to the distortion or destruction of the original, deserve Hamlet's caustic censure: "That's villainous and shows a most pitiful ambition in the fool that uses it" (III, ii, 40-41).

How, exactly, does Shakespeare present Lafew, and what does he tell us about him? We see him first, clad in deep mourning like the others on the stage, reassuring the widowed Countess of Rossillion that the King of France will be as a husband and protector to her and as a father to young Ber-

17. Richard David, "Plays Pleasant and Plays Unpleasant," *Shakespeare Survey* 8 (1955): 135.
18. Ibid., p. 134; my italics.

tram, who now, as ward to the King, has been commanded to attend his guardian at court. His comfort is trustworthy, because Lafew is close enough to the King to have heard him talk about the great sickness that afflicts him.

Lafew appears next before the King, who is so sick that he must be led to his royal chair by attendants. In playful terms that show how completely Lafew enjoys the royal favor, he asks leave to bring in Helena. Permission granted and Helena presented, Lafew departs with a mildly scandalous—and unreproved—reference to himself as a pander.

The third scene of act II opens with Lafew's report of the almost miraculous healing of the King and then shows him more nimble-witted than Parolles in their first encounter. At once the King enters and calls in his wards so that Helena may choose a husband. We, the audience, know what her decision will be and admire the poise with which she disqualifies the first four, one by one. Standing too far off to hear the words that are being spoken, Lafew watches the haughty young nobles, who in their pride—except perhaps for a quite young boy—want none of Helena and voices his indignation and disgust at the degeneracy of French youth. When only Bertram is left, Lafew weighs and labels him:

> There's one grape yet; I am sure thy father drunk wine—but if
> thou be'st not an ass, I am a youth of fourteen; I have known
> *(II, iii, 97-99)* thee already.

And, sure enough, Bertram is much too proud to wish to mingle his blood with that of a mere physician's daughter. He acquiesces only upon a direct threat by the King.

Up to this point, the audience may be uncertain about Parolles. In act I, in the house of mourning, he had appeared as a flash of life and color. His conversation with Helena, a disquisition on Virginity—a sort of pale imitation of Falstaff upon Honor—shows that he pretends to wit and worldly wisdom. But Shakespeare had undercut the impression Parolles wishes to make through Helena's words as she sees him come on stage:

> I love him for [Bertram's] sake;
> And yet I know him a notorious liar,
> *(I, i, 93-95)* Think him a great way fool, solely a coward.

At court, Parolles affects the patronizing role of veteran soldier to the young French lords about to go to the wars and presumes to tutor young Bertram in social conduct. As we saw earlier, Lafew took his measure readily in the exchange of comments about the healing of the King. But to make all sure for the audience, Shakespeare brings the men together again, and there can be no doubt about the justness of Lafew's contempt for Parolles and for the latter's vainglorious pretense of social equality with Count Bertram; nor can there be doubt that Parolles is a coward. This colloquy is advance warning of Bertram's folly in listening to Parolles, and it prepares us to believe Lafew when, almost at once, with Parolles present, he tells Bertram that "the soul of this man is his clothes; trust him not in matter of heavy consequence" (II, v, 42-44).

As the action moves to its close, Lafew is at Rossillion again, this time to mollify the displeasure of the Countess toward Bertram by throwing most of the blame on Parolles. Then he tells her that in an effort to restore Bertram in the King's favor he has asked his majesty to favor a match between Bertram and the daughter of Lafew. Such a union had been suggested by the King years before, when the couple were still in their minority. The King has favored the proposal, and now the Countess gives her approval. Then she requests Lafew to remain at Rossillion until the King and Bertram meet again.

Meanwhile, the utterly disgraced Parolles, like the Prodigal Son, has come to himself. There is no father for him to return to, and so, as if by instinct, he turns to Lord Lafew.

Parolles: O my good lord, you were the first that found me.
. . . .
It lies in you, my lord, to bring me in some grace, for you did bring me out.
Lafew. Out upon thee, knave! ... Sirrah, inquire further after me; I had talk of you last night. Though you are a fool and a knave, you shall eat . . . .
Parolles: I praise God for you.   *(V, ii, 41-53)*

And well he may do so. Where else would he have found compassion?

There is Lafew, a fount of dignity and integrity; wise, shrewd, with eyes that look quite through the deeds of men.

From Lavatch, "a shrewd knave and an unhappy," to Parolles, to Bertram, to Helena, and the King, he knows them all and serves as an infallible touchstone for the audience.

What I have been trying to say is a commonplace. So much has been written about Shakespeare that a man must be a confirmed optimist to hope to say anything new. At best, he can hope he has been dull in a new way. I would remind you that in Shakespeare there are characters so typical, so simply functional, as to exist almost in one dimension. At the other extreme, Hotspur, Falstaff, Hamlet, Lear seem as three-dimensional as our very selves. In between there are all gradations. Some, like Lafew, are witnesses for the crown or the defense, or both, but witnesses whom Shakespeare has taken the trouble to make absolutely credible. The critic, the actor, the director who ignores or distorts or perverts the documentation Shakespeare has given him must actually consider himself a better playwright than Shakespeare.

I hope all is well with Lafew—at least, he escaped having Bertram for a son-in-law!

The Invulnerability of Evil 7

CLIFFORD LEECH

Let us begin by looking at the last words of *Othello*. When the Moor has stabbed himself, Lodovico begins the terrible coda:

Lod: O bloody period!
Gra: All that's spoke is marr'd.
Oth: I kiss'd thee ere I kill'd thee; no way but this,
                    [*Falling upon* Desdemona]
Killing myself to die upon a kiss.
Cas: This did I fear, but thought he had no weapon;
    For he was great of heart.
Lod: [*To* Iago]   O Spartan dog!
More fell than anguish, hunger, or the sea.
Look on the tragic loading of this bed;
This is thy work; the object poisons sight;
Let it be hid. Gratiano, keep the house,
And seize upon the fortunes of the Moor,
For they succeed on you. To you, lord governor,
Remains the censure of this hellish villain,
The time, the place, the torture; O, enforce it.
Myself will straight aboard, and to the state
This heavy act with heavy heart relate.[1]

(V, ii, 355-70)

There could hardly be a more dreadful ending of a play. All that Lodovico can do is to tell Iago to look on the destruction he has done, Gratiano to take over Othello's possessions, and Cassio to see to Iago's protracted death. Tillyard has told us that a Shakespearean tragedy ends with a movement upward

---

1. Quotations from Shakespeare are from the one-volume Oxford edition, edited by W. J. Craig (London, 1935).

from disaster,[2] but what amelioration can we find here? Astonishingly, the villain still lives, as nowhere else in Jacobean tragedy; of course, he will soon die in agony, for what that is worth, but he has outlived Othello and Desdemona and his own wife who denounced him. And when he is dead, there is no guarantee at all that the principle he stands for will not resurrect itself. "He hath a daily beauty in his life / That makes me ugly," said Iago concerning the very ordinary Cassio: that makes us recognize the animus that the man devoted to evil feels toward the simple man who, despite his imperfection, "belongs." It is also a measure of the distance that ordinary men feel between themselves and the man who totally recognizes himself as "evil." That was how Hamlet saw Claudius. Of course, it is not how we see him. We may not go so far as Wilson Knight in regarding Hamlet as a nuisance in Elsinore, a young man who got in the way of a competent king—a usurper yet a good politician in dealing with Fortinbras, with the capacity to bring Hamlet to reason if Hamlet had let him.[3] We can nevertheless see Claudius as a being quite apart from Hamlet's vision of him, a man who could have managed despite his guilt, if only Hamlet had been prepared to wait for the succession. And let us not be puritanical about Claudius's drinking habit: about two years later the King of England and Scotland and King Christian of Denmark, when he visited England, seem to have outdone Claudius. It may not be too hazardous to guess that, in this respect, Shakespeare was projecting onto Claudius something that he feared for himself.

But Hamlet could not wait. Not only did he resent the overhasty marriage and the "incest" (which in the play only he and the Ghost refer to: everyone else seems to find the marriage as acceptable as England found Henry VIII's marriage to his elder brother's widow), but he felt impatient about the usurpation, speaking later in the play of how Claudius had "Popp'd in between the election and my hopes." But after the initial shock came the Ghost's revelation of the murder and the adultery: from then on Claudius is for him total evil, a satyr compared with that Hyperion his father. So he has to try

2. E. M. W. Tillyard, *Shakespeare's Last Plays* (London, 1938), pp. 16-18.

3. See *The Wheel of Fire* (London, 1930), chaps. 2 and 3.

to goad himself into action, despite a difficulty that he himself recognizes but cannot explain. In talking with Horatio in V, ii, he lists the affronts that Claudius has offered him, and asks for moral support in the taking of action:

Does it not, thinks't thee, stand me now upon—
He that hath kill'd my king and whor'd my mother,
Popp'd in between the election and my hopes,
Thrown out his angle for my proper life,
And with such cozenage—is't not perfect conscience
To quit him with this arm? and is't not to be damn'd
To let this canker of our nature come
In further evil?   *(V, ii, 63-70)*

It is interesting that the climactic point here is that Claudius has tried to kill Hamlet himself, and with "cozenage." There is indignation here of a special kind. Hamlet is whipping himself up, substituting for Claudius's "incest" and murder the attempt on his own life as the main cause of resentment. Even so, he waits for Providence to act. The man is too evil even now, it seems, to be touched. He and Claudius are "mighty opposites," he declares. The nether pole has a measure of invulnerability: it can hardly be reached. He is sure of his own virtue, which in the closet scene he asked Gertrude to forgive him for. The "mighty opposites" have become total emblems, for him, of Vice and Virtue. He recognizes Claudius as Michael might bow, even if disdainfully, to Satan in Byron's *The Vision of Judgment*.

There is nothing entirely new in Shakespeare here. We may think of Titus Andronicus shooting arrows against Heaven after his enemies have been guilty of the rape and mutilation of Lavinia, the murder of two of Titus's sons, the trick to make Titus cut off his hand. Here, I believe, the early play anticipates what was to come to full splendor later. In the time of that full splendor we have Lear's feeble threat against Goneril and Regan:

                No, you unnatural hags,
I will have such revenges on you both
That all the world shall—I will do such things,
What they are yet I know not, but they shall be
The terrors of the earth. You think I'll weep;

No, I'll not weep:
I have full cause of weeping, but this heart
Shall break into a hundred thousand flaws
(II, iv, 281-89) Or ere I'll weep. O fool! I shall go mad.

Of course, he can do nothing. So Othello said of Iago, when he recognized him as a "devil": "If thou be'st a devil, I cannot kill thee," and so too there is Iago's proud reply: "I bleed, sir, but not kill'd." The "sir" here is splendid: Iago ironically recognizes their former relationship, but defiantly takes to himself the status of "devil," one beyond the mortal wounding of Othello's sword. Of course, as we have seen, after the play is done, he will die in agony. But, taking the word "devil" to himself, he mockingly accepts the implication that he may suffer but cannot die. In the ultimate sense he is right: one may kill the evil man, but that does not rid the world of evil.

The men and women committed to evil in Shakespeare are often killed in a mysterious fashion: Macbeth dies at the hands of another mortal man, but a man specially privileged through his way of birth; Edmund dies through the intervention of an unnamed and disguised adversary, who is only later recognized as his half brother; Goneril and Regan can die only by suicide or through the other's plotting, evil here destroying evil.

So one reason—only one, I have to insist—why Hamlet cannot kill Claudius is that the man who, for the avenger, represents the total idea of evil is in an important sense invulnerable. He may be killed only when the avenger knows that death for himself is imminent: when no longer does anything matter except the now unqualified impulse to revenge, and a sudden strength may come with the sense of freedom bestowed by the prospect of immediate death. It may already be evident that I do not wish to discount either the Freudian interpretation of Ernest Jones in his book *Hamlet and Oedipus*,[4] which sees Hamlet's inhibition as arising from his measure of identification with Claudius as Gertrude's lover, or the existentialist idea that one can break through to full existence most easily when death is close, as with Matthieu in the final volume of Sartre's *Les Chemins de la liberté*. I am here suggesting, however, that the play *Hamlet* presents us with a whole

4. London, 1949.

group of reasons for the delay and the ultimate action, and
that one of these is the dreadfully inhibiting nature of total
evil when one feels its presence in a particular person. And
have not we all felt that? We may have felt it in relation to a
mere university administrator when, like Claudius, he was
simply trying to hold on to his job.

Yet Marlowe did not see things in this way. His Tamburlaine and Faustus came to their ends because the gods (whatever they were) decreed it. His Jew, his Edward, his Guise, his
Dido, had to suffer because men brought them to their fates.
He never saw a man confronted with the terrible problem of
killing a representative of total evil: his Tamburlaine and
Faustus and Edward exhibit only extreme folly, and even their
greatest cruelty has a casualness about it. Others may see them
as adversaries, but not as total evil: Tamburlaine in his treatment of his captives, Faustus in his pranks in the Vatican, are
too absurdly presented to be seen as providing an ultimate.
The kind of situation I have been referring to is, I believe,
specially though not exclusively Shakespearean. But it is not
to be found in the early Shakespeare, apart from the hint in
Titus Andronicus that I have mentioned. The *Henry VI* plays
and *Richard III* show us evil enough, culminating in the
bravura personality of Richard of Gloucester himself, but in
these plays it is possible for their contemporaries to get the
better of evil's representatives without scruple or hesitation; in
fact, fate seems to ally itself with the adversaries of evil, however slowly it may manifest itself. As soon as Richard wins the
crown, he feels it slipping away, and although he makes a
grand show at the end he is manifestly vulnerable—vulnerable
both to the curse of Queen Margaret and to the concerted
action of his adversaries.

But if what I have been talking about is not found in Marlowe or in the early Shakespeare, neither is it found in Shakespeare's immediate successors or close contemporaries. Vindice
in *The Revenger's Tragedy* takes delight in exterminating his
"nest of dukes": though he takes on something of their evil as
he perpetrates his revenge, he and his brother can be killed at
the end in a quite casual manner; the revengers in Webster's
The White Devil are sure, quite simply, that they are right to
kill Vittoria and Bracciano and Flamineo, however dubious we

may feel about the revengers' own virtue; Ferdinand in *The Duchess of Malfi* has his sister killed because he loves her, not because she is evil, and he himself is ignominiously killed by accident, "in a mist."

The existentialist ideas of killing and dying are no longer strange to us. In the writing of the last hundred years we have many examples of men who "come to themselves" only when death is imminent. I have referred already to Matthieu in *Les Chemins de la liberté*. We may think also of Master Builder Solness in Ibsen's *The Master Builder*, of his John Gabriel Borkman, who finally breaks free from his prison to go into the open air, climbs the hill, and dies in the snow in freedom, of his protagonist in *When We Dead Awaken* who goes ever higher into the mountains, finally enduring the avalanche that awaits him. So too we can think of Malcolm Lowry's novel *Under the Volcano*, where the ex-consul comes ultimately to be thrust down into the ravine, paradoxically achieving in ignominious death a kind of willed ending that he could never have had in living with his wife Yvonne and his brother Hugh.

There is, however, another way in which evil can be presented as invulnerable. This is not to embody it in a particular character, or even to see it as embodied in another character from the point of view of the protagonist, but to see it as becoming impersonally dominant, indeed overriding, in the circumstances of the action. The evil in *King Lear* is in some measure embodied in Goneril and Regan, Cornwall and Edmund, but all these figures become petty before the end: ultimately with more importance it is found in the nature of things as posited in the play.

This shift in *King Lear* is just possibly to be found also in *Paradise Lost*. The degeneration of Satan in the poem is commonly referred to, and when he and the lesser devils are reduced to serpents in Book 10, the reader may feel that the evil cause that he has so vigorously championed no longer truly belongs to him. Just as Goneril and Regan are finally mere squabblers for Edmund's love, and evil belongs then more essentially to the whole nature of things, so—whatever Milton's conscious intention—Satan is reduced to the level of a mere instrument of an unknowable principle. In this suggestion, the

influence of William Empson's book *Milton's God*[5] will be
apparent. The idea is of course by no means explicit in Milton,
and in *King Lear* it is not firmly asserted. Nevertheless, it
seems implicit in Lear's basic question: "Is there any cause in
nature that makes these hard hearts?" We come much nearer
to the explicit in the nihilistic vision that belongs to Macbeth
when, at the end of his play, he has given up referring to the
loss of his "eternal jewel." Even so, *Lear* and *Macbeth* are
plays where certain characters have consciously embraced evil.

What we can also find, in some plays and films of this
century, is the presentation of ineluctable evil as wholly con-
ditioning the lives of the people involved although the people
themselves are at worst fumbling, at their best strong in their
straining after the good. The three characters in Sartre's *Huis
clos* are imperfect enough, cowardly and cruel in a petty way,
but they did not invent the Second Empire room where they
are to torment one another during an indefinite future. The
major films of Ingmar Bergman and Luis Buñuel give us even
clearer instances of this approach to the idea of a basic and
indomitable evil. For Bergman we can most profitably refer to
the trilogy consisting of *Through a Glass Darkly*, *Winter Light*,
and *The Silence*, which deal respectively with the onset of an
incurable insanity, with the loss of faith in divine providence
and in human love, and with an ever-increasing difficulty in
communication that threatens to become total. Here there are
no villains, only people unable to do other than recognize the
impenetrability of the encompassing wall. The first of the
three films, *Through a Glass Darkly*, has a slightly sanguine
moment at the very end, where it appears that the encounter
with another person's suffering may bring that person's inti-
mates more closely together—an idea that Graham Greene
made use of in his play *The Living Room*. There is no such
sanguineness in *Winter Light* or *The Silence*: they present the
evil that constricts and ultimately destroys when the barriers
have become total. So, I think, quite uniformly, do the major
films of Luis Buñuel.

In the presentation of characters who through their very

5. London, 1961.

evil seem proof, at least for a time, against destruction, there is
something that belongs deeply in the Judaeo-Christian tradition. God does not, apparently cannot, annihilate Satan or
Cain and even gives Cain his safeguard. In more recent years
we have Ibsen's button-molder in *Peer Gynt*, who talks easily
about melting down the men who have not fully made themselves either for good or for evil. Milton's Satan, we remember,
indicates a preference for hell over nonexistence: in that he
joins hands with Sisyphus as Camus saw him. And we have to
recognize Macbeth as qualifying for something more than the
ladle—though, as ever, Shakespeare makes no pronouncement
as to his destination after death. In Noel Coward's *Private
Lives* the man and woman talked rather sadly of their belief in
"a rather gloomy merging into everything" after death: it was
what the button-molder offered an alternative to, but he did
not promise it was easy. The man who lives up to "Evil, be
thou my good" achieves a distinction that equals that of the
saint: Judas and Brutus and Cassius are ignominiously treated
in Dante's hell, but there is something to be said for being in
the lowest circle of all.

But it is not merely in Judaeo-Christian thought that a
special privilege seems granted to those truly distinguished in
evil. Why did Medea, having killed her children and her Jason's
new wife, get away scot-free through divine intervention? Why
was Oedipus, so guilt-ridden, welcomed by Theseus as holy,
though inadmissable to the city of Athens? A sense of sacred-
ness can indeed go along with a sense of supreme evil. Perhaps
I can illustrate this best from Shakespeare's *Macbeth*. I have
argued elsewhere that the man devoted to evil achieves a degree of awareness that he would never have known if he had
been content with winning "golden opinions" through the
ability to "unseam" an enemy "from the nave to the chaps."[6]
Macbeth does indeed grow beyond this: we need not accept
his wholly nihilistic vision ("it is a tale / Told by an idiot, full
of sound and fury, / Signifying nothing"), nor I think does
Shakespeare press this on us, wanting us merely to see it as a
state of mind that a man may be forced into; nevertheless, this
is an intensely experienced vision of the universe that tran-

6. "The Dark Side of *Macbeth*," *The Literary Half-yearly*
(Mysore), January and July 1967.

scends what the good fighter of I, iii could have reached. Webster took his Duchess of Malfi near to this when she cursed the stars, but with her the fit was momentary. She was devout, and on her knees, though still commendably arrogant, when she died. Macbeth's case is different, for he never retracts—even though he is dreadfully tired of evil, not wanting to kill Macduff after having killed the man's wife and children. The unrelenting practice of evil has made him feel sick of it—a lesson he could have learned in no other way. To say that a man has grown through the embracing of evil is a hard doctrine: it is no wonder that after this play Shakespeare turned back to Plutarch to find a less anguishing—though, it turned out, no less reliable—basis for tragedy.

Outside tragedy, but commonly referred to in tragic writing, are those mythical figures who are singled out for special torment in the pagan underworld: Tantalus, Ixion, Sisyphus. In general the underworld was seen by the Greeks and Romans as a dim half-life, filled with regret for the world that had been lost. We remember that Achilles told Odysseus that he would sooner be the meanest slave if only he could return to earth, and that in Book 6 of the *Aeneid* the dead hold out their hands in desire for the other side of the Styx. Yet there was also the special distinction given to the ultimate rebels. As already noted, Albert Camus has turned Sisyphus into the type-figure of the man who is eternally and fully alive because eternally self-aware. He and the other great sinners have not the mere half-life of Achilles in the underworld. Sisyphus is everlastingly tormented, but the torment, the separation from mere men, gives him a special kind of security.

But let us get back to *Hamlet*. I have indicated a readiness to accept the Freudian interpretation as part, though only part, of the truth about the play: as J. I. M. Stewart has pointed out,[7] we are more fully aware of the potentialities of human anguish than Bradley was, though he indeed had strong anticipatory insights into the devastating effects of family relations. What neither Bradley nor Freud nor Jones seems to recognize is that the idea of total evil in the adversary could inhibit action. If for a moment we may look outside of literature or myth, we may wonder whether this may explain the

7. *Character and Motive in Shakespeare* (London, 1949).

docility of so many of Hitler's victims. It was, I think, what
made Medea invulnerable, and what made Claudius invulnerable until Hamlet felt his own death upon him. Then he could
feel the truly "existentialist" moment, releasing him from all
inhibition.

I have already suggested that the readers and spectators do
not see Claudius as representing total evil, but that Hamlet
did—so much so that in the last scene he could speak of himself and Claudius as "mighty opposites" and could dismiss
Rosencrantz and Guildenstern as mere pawns intervening between Claudius and himself. Such an utterance does, of course,
represent a high degree of arrogance.

There is no necessity for me to underline the fact that
Hamlet himself is not totally "evil," however badly he be-
haves: in the nunnery scene, in the play scene (where he is
truly astrocious in his words to Ophelia), in his sending Rosencrantz and Guildenstern to their deaths, "no shriving time allowed." Nor is Othello wedded to evil in killing Desdemona
and in agreeing to the death of Cassio. Nor is Lear in his
repudiation of Cordelia and in his exiling of Kent. What matters with Othello and Lear is, ultimately, their recognition of
the evil they have done: This is curiously absent from Hamlet,
who apologizes to Laertes for his behavior at the graveside but
shows no sign of guilt for the deaths of Polonius and Ophelia.
Hamlet remains indeed the most complex and most baffling of
Shakespeare's tragic heroes. But for all three of these characters the evil they have occasioned is extreme. Hamlet, for
example, has killed Polonius and Rosencrantz and Guildenstern and Laertes and Claudius, and it is through his acquies-
cence in the fencing match that Gertrude dies too. How much
of this can we forgive him for? Much more, surely, than we
can forgive Medea. And, in the Greeks' eyes, he would be
surely comparatively guiltless in comparison with Oedipus. Yet
guilty he deeply is, despite all his sanguineness in his talk with
Horatio in the beginning of V, ii. In that talk he seems to ask
for his friend's agreement that to kill Claudius is in accord
with "perfect conscience"; interestingly, Horatio does not
reply to the question, but changes the topic of conversation.

All men in tragedy, particularly the heroes, are sinners: that
is true even of Antigone, who defied Creon even while seeing

Creon's case. It has no particular relation to the Christian scheme. As I have in passing indicated above, it is surely not relevant to talk of the heroes' "damnation" (we could as well talk of the damnation of Romeo and Juliet): what matters is their frailty along with their dominance and authority. What also matters, supremely, is their inability to cope with the emblems of evil that they confront. Hamlet "makes up" his special emblem of evil: for us, Claudius is a usurper, a murderer, but a good enough king. It is a different matter with Lear: we are merely confirmed in our opinion when he recognizes his two elder daughters as truly evil by the end of act II of his tragedy. Othello has to wait till act V before he discovers what Iago has done, but we have known long before. Macbeth is the exception in embracing evil in full consciousness, and, as I have suggested, through it lives to find a fuller measure of life. But all of Shakespeare's tragic heroes, in one way or another, sin. No one can fully envy them, yet in a sense we partially can. We all live on a level below that of Hamlet, Othello, Lear, Macbeth. In the last of the four major tragedies (and in an important sense Bradley's grouping is right), we have the "villain-hero" presented in all his fated "freedom." Even so, we should note that Hamlet, Othello, and Lear all die in a special way: Hamlet through a trick, not his, which ultimately allows him to kill Claudius, Othello through suicide, Lear through a broken heart over the dead body of Cordelia. We cannot feel much happiness in any of these ends, and have to recognize that in a sense they have all killed themselves. But Macbeth stands in a special position. The difference is that he alone is opposed to the coming restorer of the kingdom's fortunes. In this he is like Richard III, like him too in recognizing that he has truly embraced evil. But Richard tried to repent, good fighter as he was to the end. Macbeth fights grandly too, but repentance no longer means anything to him.

Moreover, we may ask what the concluding speech of Malcolm in *Macbeth* truly amounts to. The "thanes" will become "earls" (for what that is worth), the supporters of "this dead butcher and his fiend-like queen" will be punished, and everyone else is welcome to the coronation at Scone. Does Malcolm, or anyone else, think that enough? Is the "idea" of Macbeth, any more than that of Iago, to be disposed of so easily? We might as well think that Falstaff can be disposed of so easily at the end of *2 Henry IV*. Of course, the man Falstaff can be dismissed, and he is indeed cruelly dismissed. When he has assured Justice Shallow:

go with me to dinner.
Come, Lieutenant Pistol; come, Bardolph:
(V, v, 94-96) I shall be sent for soon at night . . .

there is an immediate entry of the Lord Chief Justice, who declares:

Go, carry Sir John Falstaff to the Fleet;
(V, v, 97-98) Take all his company along with him.

All that Falstaff can say—and these words are the last we shall hear from him, apart from the deflated verbiage in *The Merry Wives of Windsor*—is "My lord, my lord! " Pistol can say "*Si fortuna me tormenta, spero contenta*," but Falstaff cannot talk in that dog-Latin, or cheer himself up with any tag at all. Yet to deal with Falstaff in Henry V's fashion is to deny the nature of life itself. It is absurd to think of getting rid of the idea of Iago, even through a protracted death for the man himself; it is equally absurd to think of banishing the idea of Falstaff. He represents the basic and eternal principle of disorder, though of a friendly sort, which will show itself in a less friendly fashion in the realm of the future Henry V. He is essentially not to be got rid of, and in the early scenes of the following play the new king will be aware of the need to kill his friends. Later he will have Bardolph killed too, but the wretched Pistol will endure: there are some people invulnerable through our contempt, not because of any awe we feel in relation to them. Earlier, at the end of *2 Henry IV* the new king has the dubious compliment of being praised by Prince John of Lancaster who so egregiously equivocated at Gaultree Forest: Falstaff's symbolizing of disorder is paralleled by the political amorality of Prince Hal's brother: Prince John represents disorder within the establishment, which is surely in the end the greater evil.

The world goes on, but evil continues. That is what all Shakespeare's tragedies and histories and tragicomedies present to us. In *Measure for Measure* Duke Vincentio pardons everyone except Lucio, who has slandered him. But this sovereign prince has in no way solved the problem of relating justice to mercy. There is a better lesson presented in the still surviving London coronation procession, where the blunt sword of mercy and the sharp sword of justice are carried side by side. When evil, however, is paramount, there is a major problem. Hamlet saw it in Claudius; Lear more justifiably (for his play is much less of a psychological demonstration) in Goneril and Regan, and Gloucester found it in Edmund; Othello only at almost the last gasp in Iago. Magnificently, Shakespeare presented his protagonist Macbeth as the evil person himself, winning a kind of greatness through his assumption of hell's mantle.

Shakespeare never thereafter went into deeper anguish than this. His Antony and Coriolanus and Timon[8] are frail: they recognize evil in their environments, but never find it in themselves. The ancient world offered him figures who, flawed as they were, had the idea of magnanimity about them. From *Hamlet* to *Macbeth* his protagonists ventured ever further into evil. He presented—in Hamlet, Lear, Othello—a clash between his flawed central figure and an antagonist or antagonists seen by that figure as truly evil, and showed how such a man could react to such a situation; in Macbeth he showed how a man wedded to evil could nevertheless attain a measure of greatness in the destruction of himself and others. After that, he presented heroes who lived in a world more corrupt than they were, but the world's corruption in *Antony and Cleopatra* and *Coriolanus* and *Timon of Athens* is of a fairly petty sort. Rome and Athens are shown to be shabby enough, but they do not seem to embody the idea of a totally destructive evil. Antony and Coriolanus and Timon are destroyed because they make mistakes in their dealings with other men. There is rivalry between one man and another, not a sense that an enemy embodies total evil.

8. I am assuming here a date of ca. 1607-8 for *Timon of Athens*: see E. K. Chambers, *William Shakespeare: A Study of Facts and Problems* (Oxford, 1930), 1:271, 483; also my *Shakespeare's Tragedies and Other Studies in Seventeenth Century Drama* (London, 1950), pp. 113-14. In my view its close relation to *Coriolanus*, in source and plot pattern, seems conclusive.

Hamlet is the earliest English tragedy of the seventeenth century, the play that made the way for Shakespeare's later tragedies and for all the other tragedies up to the closing of the theaters in 1642. It is, moreover, a play that includes within its scope the discussion of many themes that were evidently matters with which Shakespeare was strongly preoccupied at this time: ghost-lore, revenge, suicide, the right way of acting a play (with a strong sense of the changes that had taken place in writing and acting since his career began), madness, the varieties and tensions of personal relationships. Scholars differ as to whether the play was first acted in 1600 or in 1601. It seems likely that it was written quite slowly, its composition having been in his mind for some time and having been actually begun two or three years before it reached the stage. In a work that has obviously been so fully considered, it is not surprising that his mind came to dwell on the idea that total evil, seen or even merely imagined, should seem invulnerable. Certainly the idea does not show itself properly in his earlier writing or in the writing of his predecessors in the drama. I have mentioned Titus's shooting his arrows against heaven because for a time Saturninus seems beyond his reach. To this may be added the frustration that Hieronimo in Kyd's *Spanish Tragedy* feels when he for a time does not see a way to get redress for the killing of his son. But for both Titus and Hieronimo the inhibition is passing: both soon become active schemers, when their wills are stiffened up, in the carrying out of revenge. And in Shakespeare's other early essay in the tragic, *Romeo and Juliet*, there is no truly evil person (Tybalt is merely a "prince of cats," an unruly young man), and the heavens or the fates are never more than vaguely thought of. The stars "cross" the lovers, but seem as concerned with ending the feud as with dealing out death. The tragic note is on occasion struck in the English histories of the 1590s, most notably in *Richard II* and *Richard III*. But Bolingbroke is a mere politician, not grand enough to be seen, even by Richard, as fully embracing evil. And the other Richard, he of Gloucester, accomplished evildoer as he is, becomes immediately vulnerable when he has won the crown. With Hamlet in relation to Claudius, Othello in relation to Iago, Lear in relation to Goneril and Regan, we have a different situation. There is nothing to be done when one is confronted by evil of this magnitude. In *Othello* and *King Lear* the protagonists are helpless against their antagonists: when the antagonists die (Iago outside the play), it is because others have acted, not the protagonists. Yet Hamlet does of course finally kill Claudius. That, however, is only when his own death is on him, when Gertrude is dead too, when the realization of the imminent end gives him a sense of freedom, and of truly major anger against the man who has caused it. I have noted that in his earlier talk with Horatio in this last scene he had shown a climactic indignation against Claudius because his own life had been put in danger, "And with such cozenage." Now Claudius has made a second attempt, and Gertrude (whose very life was a further source of inhibition) is already dead. He can have his "existentialist" moment, as Matthieu has been seen to have at the end of Sartre's *Les Chemins de la liberté*.

In relation to all this, it seems legitimate to offer a comment on Hamlet's behavior in the "prayer scene." If there is any validity at all in the argument I have presented in this paper, we shall not take his words at their face value. It is deeply ironic that, as soon as Hamlet has left his uncle still alive, Claudius tells us that he cannot properly pray because he cannot give up his kingdom and his queen, the fruits of his sin. Claudius is a better theologian than Hamlet here. But surely Hamlet knew his moral theology as well as Claudius did; surely he knew that the murderer-usurper-adulterer could not exculpate himself merely by praying? Moreover, if we believed that Hamlet truly wanted to ensure Claudius's damnation, we should be putting him on the level of Esdras of Grenado in Nashe's *The Unfortunate Traveller*, where the revenger—who wanted to ensure his victim's damnation by getting him to abjure God by promising him life, only to shoot him in the throat so that he might not recant his abjuration—aroused horror among those who heard of his deed. Rather, Hamlet is finding an excuse, as so often before he had done, for inaction. The man is at his mercy, but the man is too evil to kill.

Who could kill Adolf Hitler except Hitler himself? It was poetically right that he was not brought to Nuremberg. Who could kill Claudius except Hamlet at the moment of death? Who could kill Edmund in *King Lear* except an unnamed ad-

versary? Who could kill Regan except Goneril? How could
Goneril die except by suicide? Who could kill Iago within the
time of the play?

Yet we have to recognize a further complexity: does any
man in actuality say "Evil, be thou my good"? Does not the
worst tyrant, the man who massacres on the grand scale, tell
himself that he is justified in doing so? We may think of twentieth-century examples and ask ourselves whether they did not
feel justification: such examples range from the good family
man Nicholas Romanov to much more deliberate despots or
demagogues of recent times. The image of total evil in a man
is, I strongly believe, a literary construct: from Richard III to
Claudius (if only in Hamlet's view), to Goneril and Regan, to
Iago, and from them to the anguished, self-tormenting Macbeth. Indeed Macbeth is a special case: he is the only one
among them who did not enjoy evil, and for that reason he
gained all the more stature through it. It is literature that has
truly envisaged evil, because in ourselves we find it potentially.
Thus literature has projected out of ourselves the realization of
a tendency that is deep within us. If—only if—we were free
from the moral sanctions that hold us in, we should be free
and invulnerable, like the men whom we truly regard as evil
because we do not understand them, because they do not fully
understand themselves. Men in actuality are too weak to be
wholly Macbeths, women too weak to be Gonerils. But writers, preeminently Shakespeare and Blake, can imagine such
things realized. If they came truly to pass, no one could stand
against them. The ultimate invitation to despair would come if
we believed in Satan.

Beyond *Hamlet* the matter goes further in Shakespeare. We
are puzzled by the wholesale pardons at the end of *Measure
for Measure*. In this play I have suggested that the ending is
unsatisfactory because Duke Vincentio has not come to terms
with the justice-mercy dichotomy. If we dispense pardons to
Mistress Overdone, Pompey, Barnardine, Angelo—Claudio is an
easier case—are we not, as governors, abdicating? Certainly it is
abdication if we remember that Vincentio withdrew from his
governorship in order that rule in Vienna might be more strict,
where he indeed saw in his dukedom

> corruption boil and bubble
> Till it o'er-run the stew. . . . *(V, i, 316-17)*

But he cannot properly cope with this. His weakness as a governor is demonstrated most fully when the only man he ultimately punished (apart from his forcing a marriage on Angelo) is Lucio, who, he says, deserves his bizarre punishment of marrying Kate Keepdown because he slandered a prince. The wretched man seems to have forced marriages on his mind, like the King of France in *All's Well That Ends Well*, who ought to have learned better than to offer Diana any husband she might choose at the play's end. The Duke in *Measure for Measure* surely gives up, as the King of France more easily does in *All's Well*. In a more anguished way Prospero abandons the task of reforming evil. He tells Antonio and Sebastian:

> But you, my brace of lords, were I so minded,
> I hear could pluck his highness' frown upon you,
> And justify you traitors: at this time
> I will tell no tales. *(V, i, 126-29)*

But he lets them go, though they show no sign of repentance. For Caliban he has to admit: "this thing of darkness I / Acknowledge mine." That is equivalent to saying that he feels Caliban's evil to be part of his own frailty, and he half-promises immunity to the witch's son. Much earlier, in *Much Ado about Nothing*, Shakespeare allowed Don John to escape: that was a comedy of a sort, and bringing the manifest villain to punishment would have brought in a truly discordant note. One has to hope that evil will just go away, or be converted as Duke Frederick was in *As You Like It*. So Malvolio in *Twelfth Night* departed with mere empty talk of revenge. But he did indeed see his persecutors as evil, and his "I'll be reveng'd on the whole pack of you!" is anticipatory in its futility of Lear's:

> I will have such revenges on you both
> That all the world shall—I will do such things,
> What they are yet I know not, but they shall be
> The terrors of the earth. *(II, iv, 282-85)*

We do not know when *Twelfth Night* was first performed: it may have been after *Hamlet*, for we know that the comedy was performed at the Middle Temple on 2 February 1602: that was not "twelfth night," so it was doubtless previously given elsewhere, though perhaps not long before. In any event, the "Madly-Used Malvolio" (as he signs his letter to Olivia) has seen his adversaries as truly evil, giving us perhaps an echo of Hamlet's mistake. So he can only talk, as Hamlet did for the great length of his play. Malvolio did not have the advantage, as Hamlet did, of both knowing death was upon him and of becoming aware of a totally affronting attempt on his own life.

Yet even Hamlet did not experience the total invulnerability of evil. He could at the end kill Claudius. It was in the tragedies after that that Shakespeare presented Othello and Lear as incapable of acting against the evil that confronted them. And in both those tragedies he did, I think, imply that evil dies only to live again: there is no security for Venice or for Britain when Iago and Goneril and Regan and Edmund and Cornwall are dead. And when Macbeth dies we have a loss of splendor: the world is the poorer without him. It is good for Scotland to be without him, but our sense of his loss is anguishing. The full existence of evil is one of the things we live with, even if we do not truly see it embodied in an individual man. And, though we may kill its apparent representative, it dies to live again. That is one of the dimly hinted at "lessons"—if there are indeed "lessons" for tragedy to give—that tragedy invites us to consider.

MILTON CRANE is professor of English at The George Washington University. He is the author of *Shakespeare's Prose* and has edited Shakespeare's *Henry VI, Part Three* and several volumes of short stories and poetry.
[1973]